More
FASCINATING
Conversion
STORIES

Books by Samuel Fisk

Forty Fascinating Conversion Stories

More Fascinating Conversion Stories

More FASCINATING Conversion STORIES

Compiled by
SAMUEL FISK

kregel
PUBLICATIONS

Grand Rapids, MI 49501

More Fascinating Conversion Stories compiled by Samuel Fisk.

Copyright © 1994 by Kregel Publications.

Published by Kregel Publications, a division of Kregel, Inc., P.O. Box 2607, Grand Rapids, MI 49501. Kregel Publications provides trusted, biblical publications for Christian growth and service. Your comments and suggestions are valued.

Editorial Assistance: Helen Bell
Cover Design: Art Jacobs
Book Design: Alan G. Hartman

Library of Congress Cataloging-in-Publication Data

Fisk, Samuel.
More fascinating conversion stories/by Samuel Fisk.
    p.   cm.
    1. Conversion—Case studies. 2. Converts, Protestants—Biography. I. Fisk, Samuel. II. Title
BV4930.M56   1994   248.2'4'0922—dc20   94-13046
                                          CIP

ISBN 0-8254-2640-5 (pbk.)

1 2 3 4 5 Printing/Year 98 97 96 95 94

Printed in the United States of America

CONTENTS

PREFACE

The reader may be assured that the accounts in this volume are more than what some imaginative mind might ingenuously think up. They are much more than statistically-recorded facts of dry history. They recount the actual experiences of vibrant people who lived and struggled as fully as any of us do today.

These stories record the details of the strivings, the ups and downs, the longings, and sometimes the fallen hopes of burdened souls. All are vitally coupled with providential circumstances, the often veiled means used by a loving God in His unfailing wooing to draw the needy soul to Himself. It is very moving to read the experiences of those who have searched or longed for, perhaps for years, and have at last found the peace of soul which seemed so elusive.

It was a pleasure and a thrill to search out and bring together the stories of how various individuals, both well known and not so well known, entered into the spiritual experience without which they would never have had peace in their hearts or have been heard of by anyone else, and moreover, without which they would never have been assured of eternal life.

Just as the compiler found real joy in gathering these narratives, if the reader finds any value or encouragement in following them, it will more than repay the effort expended and will give still deeper satisfaction to know that they are in some way being used to the glory of God and the blessing of souls.

Appreciation is here expressed to the many persons who have helped in one way or another in the preparation of this work. It would be difficult to mention everyone, but particular recognition is gratefully expressed to: Dr. Robert L. Sumner of Biblical Evangelism for his long and unstinting assistance; to my faithful wife, Hilda, for corrections and encouragement; and to others who helped in manuscript preparation. Thanks is also given to the subjects whose experiences appear in this volume and to the authors, editors, and publishers who have graciously allowed their work to be used. And not least, special recognition is due to the editorial staff of Kregel Publications, without whose skillful efforts this book would never have been published.

Finally, our hope is that the total impact of these narratives will encourage many to probe the depths of their hearts and before God ask some searching questions: Do we know in personal experience the reality of what these accounts point to—the consciousness of acceptance with God and the forgiveness of sins through the work of Christ? Put it to the test—that which brings peace and blessing which, as these stories relate, so many others have found, can be found by all. And lastly, are we doing our part to share the good news, to pass the word along? May this volume help us to do so.

1

DR. WILLIAM WARD AYER:
God's Man in Manhattan

D r. William Ward Ayer, pastor of New York's Calvary Baptist Church, proclaimed the riches in Christ to millions of people both in his congregation and in his radio audience. Mel Larson, his biographer, estimated the radio audience ". . . at more than five hundred thousand who listened each Sunday to the crackling, chuckling voice of a man who was once told to stay out of the ministry for fear he would be a failure. The entire eastern part of the United States came to know and respect this unusual and dynamic man of the ministry."

One of the leading radio stations of New York (not the one over which Ayer broadcast) conducted a poll to determine the most outstanding figures of the city. To the surprise of many, even newscasters, Ayer was rated third, just after Mrs. Eleanor Roosevelt (widow of the late president), but ahead of Mayor William O'Dyer, Ex-mayor La Guardia, Bernard Baruch, John D. Rockefeller, Jr., Babe Ruth, and other notables. These facts speak for themselves about a man who never sought popular acclaim and who never preached merely to gain the masses.

The story of Dr. Ayer's conversion is a great testimony to what God can do in a life formerly set against the gospel. We take it from *God's Man in Manhattan* by Mel Larson.

11

"A printer living a careless life, a boy who drank periodically with his goodhearted but loose-living friends, was working in Boston. Billy Sunday, an evangelist, had come to Boston, erected his huge tabernacle, and was preaching to that Roman Catholic-dominated metropolis. The whole city was stirred. . . .This meant nothing to Willie who was twenty-four. Ayer was endeavoring to lead a respectable life, but religion had no interest for him. An outspoken agnostic, he read much anti-religious literature. He was keenly interested in union labor affairs and was being groomed for union leadership.

"When Billy Sunday 'dared' to come to Boston, Ayer told his printing buddies, 'He's a fake.' Ayer's sister Abigail was a Christian and was interested in his becoming one. She invited him to the meetings, but he only laughed at her.

"One day a campaign petition came through the Ginn Printing Co. where Ayer worked. One of Sunday's methods was to have workers from factory groups attend the meetings together. Ginn and Co. was given a Saturday night, and the petition for signatures of those who would attend was sent through the composing room.

"Roman Catholics working in the shop made a mockery of the petition. They signed fictitious names and added insulting words. Ayer knew the petition was coming, and he did not intend to sign it. However, something happened to him when the petition was placed before him, and he saw the joke the Catholics had made of it. His Protestant blood boiled. He took the petition and tore it into bits. Then he obtained another, signed his own name at the top, and went through the composing room with it. 'Sign it if you're going,' he said, 'and no uncomplimentary remarks.'

"Ayer's circulating the petition meant one thing. He himself was now obligated to attend the meeting. He did not care to go, but he thought it would be an unusual way to spend Saturday night. Ayer did not believe a word that Sunday said, but he was conscious of his sincerity and earnestness. As he made his way home, Ayer felt that he wanted to come again if only to better understand this 'fanatic,' who at least had the power to nearly turn the city upside down.

"The next meeting he chose to attend was a 'For Men Only' gathering on a Sunday afternoon. It was a most unusual service; between ten and twelve thousand men jammed the great tabernacle. Sunday preached his famous baseball sermon, telling the story of his life and comparing what God had done for him with what had happened to a number of other White Sox players who had been with him that afternoon he had sat on a Chicago curbstone listening to the testimonies of an open-air group from the Pacific Garden Mission. His dramatic closing illustration of the heavenly Umpire calling some out and some safe gripped the great throng and held them spellbound."

All this time there were other unseen influences of which Ayer was hardly aware. Going back, we read, "His conversion, humanly speaking, may be said to date back to the praying mother. Once or twice when he had come home slightly intoxicated to his brother's home, he was reminded, 'And to think that you were the one Mother said would be a minister.' Ayer would laugh and say, 'Well, Mother was old-fashioned and didn't know much.' . . .

"A second thread in the pattern of Ayer's conversion was his sister Abigail. It was to this Abbie to whom Ayer as a lonesome lad had been attached after the death of their mother. She had come to Boston and had become a Christian. When the Billy Sunday campaign was announced, she and a Miss Cruz agreed to pray daily for Ayer, trusting God that during the ten-week campaign Willie would be converted. Eight weeks of the campaign went by and still he had not attended. They continued to pray, however, feeling that God in some way would answer.

"On the very night Ayer attended the first service, after the flare-up at work caused by the petition signing, Abbie and Miss Cruz were praying for him. They were troubled because he as yet had not attended a service; when he did attend, he did not tell Abbie.

"John Murphy went with Ayer to that 'Men Only' meeting on Sunday afternoon when Ayer felt that Sunday was 'kicking me sermonically all over the place.' As they walked out of the tabernacle, Murphy asked Ayer if he would like to make a decision for Christ. Ayer said no. On Huntington Avenue they came to the Y.M.C.A. building and noticed an after-meeting going on in connection with the campaign. Persistent, Murphy said, 'Let's go in, Bill, and see what's going on.'

"The auditorium was filled with men. Isaac Ward was to speak. Before he did so he conducted a testimony meeting which proved to be Ayer's undoing. He never had seen or heard anything like it. Scores of men were on their feet, anxious to tell what Christ had done for them. A rough-looking, rough-voiced former Roman Catholic walked to the platform, Bible in hand. He told how he came to Boston, a drunken bum riding a freight train. He had gone to the tabernacle to get warm. As he told how he was converted there, his face lit up with joy. One after another, men gave their testimonies. Ward never did get to preach. These testimonies showed Ayer the power of God in men's lives.

"Something tightened in Ayer's throat. He never had felt like that before. Ward spoke closing words which Ayer never has forgotten, 'We must close, but remember, men, the question is: "What will you do with Jesus?"'

"He asked those who wished to accept Christ to stand. A few stood. Ayer was so convicted he was almost sickened. He gripped the bottom of his chair so he would not rise and declare himself. Years later he said, 'If anyone ever knew the conviction of the Holy Spirit, I knew it at that moment!' He persisted in his refusal until the meeting was dismissed. As he and Murphy walked down the stairway, Ayer had the 'lowest, meanest feeling I ever have felt.' He realized he had caught a vision of Jesus' power to save.

"The campaign was in its final week when he decided to go once more. Sunday spoke on, 'What shall the end be of them that obey not the Gospel of God?' The message dug its way into Ayer's heart. When the invitation was given, he realized it was now or never. Bucking the people who were leaving the tabernacle, he made his way down the aisle to the front. He grabbed hold of Sunday's hand with a vise-like grip.

"Ayer sat down, signed a decision card, and had prayer. Then he walked out, feeling that at least an open decision had been made and that from now on he would live a Christian life. He knew he was a sinner; he saw Jesus Christ as Savior. Now he entrusted all to Him.

"He talked to a pastor on Friday night and told him, 'Christ has come into my heart. Now I'm not concerned about the doubts which were in my mind. They're gone.'"

So Ayer was on his way—to preach Christ on more than one continent, publish books, and lift up Christ before a needy world.

Taken from *God's Man in Manhattan* by Mel Larson. Copyright © 1950, Zondervan Publishing House. Used by permission.

2

JOHN BIRCH:
A Martyr Inadequately Appreciated

For quite some time the name of John Birch has been commonly heard, whether mentioned in appreciation or with easygoing discountenance. The assumption of some has been that Mr. Birch must have been one wholly given over to campaigning for extreme right-wing causes—a view stretching things a bit beyond what actually occurred in his short life.

That, however, is not the point we wish to deal with here. We desire to treat John Birch at this time as an outstanding Christian young man, which he truly was, loyal to Christ and to his country, for which he suffered a cruel death at the hands of Chinese communists.

Too few have paused to look into what John Birch really was and what his ideals and purpose in life were. It may surprise many to know that John Birch actually was, above all, a man with a missionary vision, whose life was dedicated to spreading the gospel of Christ and His great redemption. Not many have realized that young John Birch volunteered for foreign missionary service while a student at Mercer University (where he received his B.A. degree *magna cum laude*). He went to China under the World's Fundamentalist Baptist Missionary Fellowship in 1940 and never returned.

In China, according to a brief biography by Robert Welch, his spoken Chinese "acquired a fluency possessed by few Americans." Also, he "conducted services and worked with Chinese ministers in the small churches of a wide area. Here was a preacher, burning with zeal, who really intended to preach. He went out regularly through the Japanese occupation lines to see rural congregations. . . ."

"He took little credit to himself for anything he accomplished. . . . But he put no limit to the possibilities of what a Divine Being might do through John Birch as one of that Being's worthy agents. . . . By his own understanding of the relationship of man to God, he had to be worthy in order to be chosen as one of God's instruments on earth." Again, "It is extremely doubtful if any fulltime chaplain in China conducted more religious services or preached more sermons than John Birch during the three years John wore the army uniform. . . . He preached to the Chinese, civilian or military or both, whenever and wherever there was an opportunity."

All that occurred in the face of overwhelming military responsibilities when, after being given a U.S. Army commission, he moved in short order from Lieutenant to Captain. Perhaps his most famous early exploit was the remarkable rescue of General Doolittle and his crew who had crash-landed behind enemy lines after their bombing raid on Tokyo, they being avidly sought for, of course, by the Japanese. Later, according to an article in *Saga* magazine, "he once walked 1,000 miles behind Japanese lines setting up the first radio intelligence network" monitoring Japanese positions. For these and other deeds of invaluable service he was awarded the Distinguished Service Cross, part of the citation for which read, ". . . almost continually in the field, living under the most primitive conditions and constantly in close proximity to the enemy, achieved phenomenal success." Also he was awarded the Legion of Merit "for exceptionally meritorious conduct in performance of outstanding service." Then he was recommended for the Congressional Medal of Honor posthumously.

But in all of this his real goals were never sidetracked. According to Mr. Welch, "It was his firm intention, often announced, to remain in China and resume his missionary activities once the war was over. . . . His consecration to this dream was so great and so positive that he made what must have been an extremely heavy sacrifice." Then an excerpt from the last letter John ever wrote (August 13 and 15, 1945): "Yesterday, Sunday morning. I held a service and all of my men voluntarily attended except the operator who had to stay by the transmitter. We have been holding Sunday morning services every week that I am here to lead them. . . . As long as it pleases God to use my voice for preaching His gospel, I expect to be doing that."

How, then, did John Birch come into such remarkably firm and warm personal faith in Christ? We take the story from *The Secret File on John Birch*, by James and Marti Hefley (Tyndale House, Wheaton, IL, 1980, o.p.). The place to begin, as often, is with the home life in which John grew up.

"During the Roaring Twenties traditional moral values were under trial and standards were crumbling. The Birches went to Sunday School and Church every Sunday. They read the Bible and prayed with their growing brood every evening after dinner. Breaking a commandment was not tolerated. The children were always to address elders, especially schoolteachers, with respect. . . .

"Theological battles raged in the big northern Protestant denominations. 'Modernists' reduced biblical miracles to natural occurrences and ridiculed the infallibility of the Bible. . . . Fundamentalists said Jesus was God in the flesh, the atoning Savior, and resurrected Lord who was coming again. John Birch always knew where his parents stood. They were rock-hard fundamentalists. As John's mentor, Aunt May, said, 'The world was created by the act of God. God said it, we believe it, that settles it.' When the Presbyterian church got a modernist preacher, no one was surprised when the Birches and their relatives pulled out.

"They found their niche in the West Baptist Church. The pastor was a staunch fundamentalist who believed that salvation was by the atonement of Christ, 'plus nothing, minus nothing.' Soon afterward, John made his profession of faith in Christ and was baptized. He was only seven years old at the time, but had become 'burdened' with sin. 'I would go to bed at night scared to go to sleep,' he testified later. 'I would think, "What if I should die before I wake?" I knew I was a sinner.'

"'Then one day the preacher gave an invitation, and I felt moved to confess and believe on the Lord Jesus Christ as my Lord and Savior. I went down to the front and told the preacher I was trusting in Christ and His blood for the forgiveness of sin and that I believed with all my heart. For the first time I knew that I believed in the Lord Jesus Christ. I knew I was a saved person.'

"L. L. Legters, a man destined to have a profound influence on young John Birch's life, was a promoter of missions. He was gifted with a vivid imagination and a delivery that held audiences spellbound. The tall, rangy Legters came to West Baptist Church when John Birch was eleven years old. . . . Legters was pacing along the platform, jabbing a forefinger at the adults and children in the pew. 'There are millions in Amazonia, Africa, and Asia who have never heard about Jesus. Can you hear their death wail? Will you take the gospel to them?'

"The fiery preacher invited those willing to go as missionaries to make a public commitment. John Birch sat spellbound, didn't go to the front, but a few days later his parents found a note he had left on the table: 'The Lord is calling me to the mission field. I have to answer to the death wail of the lost.' The die was cast. John Birch would be a missionary carrying the message of the Bible to the heathen. For him, the Bible would be the final authority in life. All else would be subservient." The rest of the story easily follows.

As to his service in China, it really meant little to John that General Claire Chennault came to place unqualified confidence in him and put tremendous responsibilities on him, repeatedly giving expression to highest commendations. For example, he said that about ninety percent of his downed fliers had been saved by John's rescue arrangements—the highest percentage in any war theater. He wrote, ". . . his devotion to duty was beyond anything that was expected of him. I cannot praise his work sufficiently." Brigadier General F. W. Evans wrote, "His duty was at all times extremely hazardous . . . he contributed immeasurably in bringing the war in China to a successful conclusion."

Interest now doubtless turns to how and why John Birch died. The story can briefly be told as far as is known, for many believe the facts were deliberately covered up. A newspaper correspondent wrote John's parents that, "had not the truth been suppressed, Captain Birch's death would have headlined every newspaper in the United States."

All that can be said, apparently, is that ten days after the surrender of Japan and the war was officially declared to be over, Captain Birch was put in charge of a team to go forward on a special post-military mission. On the way, it seems, they were stopped by some Chinese forces who were supposed to be our allies against the Japanese but were evidently controlled by committed communists. John and a loyal Chinese officer were separated from the rest of the group, disarmed under protest, led away, and two shots were heard. It was assumed that John had been killed by one of the shots, but a later autopsy revealed he had apparently died from repeated bayonet thrusts! Why? Probably to display that the Communists would do what they wanted—accountable to no one. Why John? Evidently because he was known to be representative of what America stood for, not excluding the Christian faith with its ideals and standards.

As to John's ideals, they shine out clearly. Departing on one of his dangerous missions, John left this message: "If anything should happen to me please tell my family I am deeply grateful for my Christian home and upbringing." Finally, in a writing four months before his death, we find these words: "I want to reach the sunset of life . . . retaining my boyhood faith in Him who promised a life to come."

May God give America many more like him!

Taken from *The Secret File on John Birch* by James and Marti Hefley. Copyright © 1980 by Tyndale House. Used by permission.

3

DAVID BRAINERD:
Developed the Spirit of Modern Missions

Why should the life of a backwoods recluse who lived two and a half centuries ago be of interest today? The answer is readily found in the posthumous influence exerted by that life.

The prominent Boston pastor, author, and educator, A. J. Gordon, said of David Brainerd: "After he was dead, William Carey read his life and went to India; Robert McCheyne read his diary and went to the Jews; Henry Martyn read his journal and went to India. . . . The marvelous missionary revival of the nineteenth century was due more to his prayers than to any other thing. . . . Brainerd was in the depths of the forests alone, unable to speak the language of the Indians. He knew he could not reach these savages; he did not understand their language. If he wanted to speak at all he must find somebody that could vaguely interpret his thought. So he spent whole days praying. What was his answer? Once he preached through a drunken interpreter, a man so intoxicated that he could hardly stand up. That was the best he could do, yet scores were converted through that sermon."

One of Brainerd's biographers introduces his subject by reporting, "When John Wesley, who had personal knowledge of the Indians, was anxious to preserve the zeal of his people, he put to his Conferences this question: 'What can be done in order to revive the work of God where it is decayed?' answering it with the emphatic counsel, 'Let every preacher read carefully over the life of David Brainerd.'"

In bringing out a later book on Brainerd, Judson Press publishers wrote that he "did more to develop the spirit of modern missions and to fire the Christian church than any other man since the apostolic age," an amazing claim.

And Oswald J. Smith of Toronto said, "So greatly was I influenced by the life of David Brainerd in the early years of my ministry that I named my youngest son after him. . . . No man ever had a greater passion for souls. To live wholly for God was his one great aim and ambition. . . . Although Brainerd did his work more than two hundred years ago, he has a message for today."

In *The Progress of World-Wide Missions*, Robert Hall Glover gives further sights. "Broken down by the hardships and exposures to which he had unfalteringly subjected himself in his long and perilous journeys and self-sacrificing labors for the Indians, he died of consumption. . . . But his short life of twenty-nine years has left behind it an influence seldom equaled in its powerful effect upon others. The memory of David Brainerd has been cherished by the most spiritual of each succeeding generation of Christians and today is still as fresh and fragrant as ever."

In reference to what he endured, the popular biographer, Richard E. Day, gave him the appellation "Flagellant on Horseback." This characterization reflects not only his physical discomforts but also his constant reaching out. Mr. Day further points out, "In the first thirty-one months of his work . . . he rode in the line of duty, 7,500 miles," and "another 7,500 miles in his last twenty-one months"—during five months of which he was confined to his bed!

While his labor for Christ did not come easily, neither did his entering into a full Christian experience come without struggle. All was characterized by agony of spirit, through which a less resolute person would have given up. From four different accounts of his life which we have, we trace the story of his conversion, all based largely on Brainerd's own recorded words. The details he left have been puzzled over by students of his life—from his contemporary Jonathan Edwards to Richard E. Day, a more recent biographer.

Part of the ambiguity may be due to the quaint Puritan New England terminology which he employed, as for example frequent references to "frames," meaning moods, or to things "secret," meaning merely not in the public eye, or to writers in those days referring confusingly to the new birth as an "effectual call." And, of course, Brainerd was not writing for twentieth century readers, not even for the eyes of others of his day. In fact, as his end drew near he ordered his journals destroyed, and only by Jonathan Edwards' intervention were they spared.

His embracing the fullness of salvation may be gathered most easily, perhaps, from an account by the biographer Jesse Page (1901). We read, "Brainerd tells us in the diary, in that portion of it which was fortunately preserved after his death, a little about his feelings at this time, and no words can better describe these days and his conversion than his own. 'I was from my youth,' he says, 'somewhat sober and inclined rather to melancholy than to the contrary extreme; but do not remember anything of conviction of sin, worthy of remark, till I was, I believe, about seven or eight years of age! Then I became concerned for my soul, and terrified at the thought of death, and was driven to the performance of duties, but it appeared a melancholy business that destroyed my eagerness for play. And though, alas, this religious concern was short-lived, I sometimes attended secret prayer, and thus lived at ease in Zion, without God in this world and without much concern, as I remember, till I was about thirteen years of age.'

"'But sometime in the winter of 1732, I was roused out of carnal security by I scarce know what means at first; but was much excited by the prevailing of a mortal sickness in Haddam [his hometown]. I felt sometimes much inclined to duties, and took great delight in the performance of them, and I sometimes hoped that I was converted, or at least in a good and hopeful way for heaven and happiness, not knowing what conversion was. I was remarkably dead to the world, and my thoughts were almost wholly employed about my soul's concerns. I was also exceedingly distressed and melancholy at the death of my mother. But afterward my religious concern began to decline and by degrees I fell back. . . .'

"The boy already seemed to be haunted with that self-condemnation and unsettlement of trust which were characteristic of the Calvinist experience of his day. He had the fear of death before his eyes and felt that the best way to obtain peace and freedom from his terrors was immersing himself in a round of duties, some, no doubt, of a painful character, in order to wean himself from love of self and of the world. Such methods, however, could not possibly have the desired result, and with his father and mother both removed to another world, he seems to have had none to point him to 'a more excellent way.' Nearly sixteen, now, the following is the retrospect of his experience, recorded in his diary:

"'About the 15th of April, I removed from my father's house where I spent four years, but still "without God in the world," though for the most part I went a round of secret duty. I was not much addicted to young company, or frolicking as it is called, but this I know, when I did go into such company, I never returned with so good a conscience as when I went; it always added new guilt.'...

"'When about twenty years of age, I applied myself to study and was now engaged more than ever in the duties of religion. I became very strict and watchful over my thoughts, words, and actions, and thought I must be sober indeed.'

"Although still profoundly dissatisfied with himself, . . . Brainerd continued to pursue a round of religious exercises and duties. In less than a year he had read the Bible twice through, gave the utmost attention to the preaching of the gospel, and snatched every moment he could for secret prayer and self-examination. . . .

"The mind of David Brainerd seems to have been perpetually set on 'frames and feelings'; he looks with fearful interest into the pool of his heart's experiences and sees there nothing but unrest and buffeting waves. . . . Thus he writes in his private diary: 'Sometime in the beginning of winter 1738 it pleased God, as I was walking out for some secret duties, to give me on a sudden such a sense of my danger and the wrath of God, that I stood amazed. From the view I had of sin and vileness I was much distressed all that day, fearing the vengeance of God would soon overtake me. I was much dejected, kept much alone, and sometimes envied the birds and beasts their happiness because they were not exposed to eternal misery as I evidently saw I was. . . . Sometimes there appeared mountains before me to obstruct my hopes of mercy, and the work of conversion appeared so great that I thought I should never be the subject of it.'

"For a long time Brainerd continued under this cloud. Like many a sincere but wretched man since his day, poor Brainerd vexed his soul with doubts as to whether he stood among the elect or not. At last, however, light came, the light of assurance, and Brainerd was for the first time filled with unspeakable joy. The Lord vouched him a glorious manifestation of His presence. He notes the day very carefully, the 12th of July, 1739, a Sunday evening, the close of a week of exceeding wretchedness, and he had, as he was wont, gone out into some solitary spot, far from men, to commune with God. The remarkable occurrence which followed, and which may be considered the hour of his conversion cannot be better told than in his own words:

"'Having been thus endeavoring to pray—though as I thought very stupid and senseless—for nearly half an hour, then as I was walking in a dark thick grove, unspeakable glory seemed to open to the view and apprehension of my soul. I do not mean any external brightness, for I saw no such thing, but it was a new inward apprehension or view that I had of God, such as I never had before. I stood still, wondered, and admired. It was widely different from all conceptions that ever I had of God or things divine. My soul rejoiced with joy unspeakable to see such a God, such a glorious Divine Being. . . . My soul was so captivated . . . that I was even swallowed up in Him. . . .'

"This moment of exceeding glory marks the spiritual starting point of David Brainerd. It [had] its roots in a firm faith in God and bore fruits of heroic endurance and righteousness. The spiritual manifestation just recorded was a real thing to Brainerd; henceforth he seems to more frequently lose sight of self, and his thoughts center more upon the will of God and his own responsibility in doing the same. . . ."

Thus we close the part we take from Jesse Page. Space forbids telling of Brainerd being at the top of his class at Yale, where he would have been valedictorian of the class but for his unjust expulsion for conviction's sake, and of his early death in the home of Jonathan Edwards.

4

DR. JOHN E. BROWN:
Evangelist, Educator, Author

During the early days of the depression, Dr. John Elward Brown's voice was familiar to thousands throughout the land, not only in great evangelistic meetings but over his widely heard radio programs. As his radio ministry developed, he brought in such men to share it as R. A. Torrey, G. Campbell Morgan, and William Evans.

Students at his Bible college, soon to become a university, were deeply impressed by Dr. Brown's stand for the truth, his gracious spirit, and his dynamic fervor. He left a lasting impression for good upon the hundreds of students who passed under his influence.

As to his evangelistic ministry, it is said that "records of his evangelism show over 400,000 decisions for Christ made in his meetings across the country." And as his radio outreach grew, it was said "he could speak to the entire nation . . . receiving mail from every state in the Union, plus Canada, Hawaii, New Zealand, and Australia."

John E. Brown's son, John Brown, Jr., gives some interesting sidelights on his father's life. "My father was a plain Iowa farm boy who knew the meaning of sunrise—for he, his father, and brothers would be about their work long before the sun came up. . . . In the small northwest Arkansas community of Rogers, he gave his heart to Christ on a cold wintery night in the year 1896. He had spent twelve hours that day working in a lime kiln, from 12:00 midnight to 12:00 noon, earning 75 cents for his twelve hours labor. The decision he made that night not only changed his life but eventually was to influence the lives of millions of people.

"With the temperature hovering around zero, sounding above the splash of rain and the howl of wind was the beat of a drum. That beat of a Salvation Army drum echoed in the ears of that 'long boy from the lime kiln' and drew my father with a strange yet compelling force to that momentous meeting. What followed was the beginning of a career in evangelism, education, and radio evangelism. . . . To his final year of 78, he was an evangelist, an educator, and author of many books." And I might add, an editor in which I assisted him."

Elsewhere it is recorded, "He became the youngest university president in the United States at age 21, when he was named to head Scarritt Collegiate Institute. This aroused in him a zeal for higher education which continued until his death."

The story of Dr. Brown's conversion is given in more detail in *John Brown of Arkansas*, by R. C. Kennedy and T. R. Rothrock. In it we read, "Sundays, as well as other days, found the Brown family at church and Elward in the choir. He inherited his love for singing from his father, and during his early ministry music played a very important part.

"By the time young John had reached his seventeenth birthday he had held many jobs and had even developed a reputation as a caller for square dances. But from the point of view of father Brown he didn't show very much promise. He certainly didn't fit the strict moral and religious codes of the family. So when John and one of his older brothers started for Arkansas, Mr. Brown commented, 'That boy will never amount to anything; we'd just as well let him go.'

"John's next and last full-time job as a laborer was at a lime kiln near Rogers. . . . One wet and chilly spring night, several of the lime kiln gang were in a cafe in Rogers, seeking what low-cost diversion the small town could offer. After a while in the stuffy atmosphere of the restaurant, John thrust his cigarette between his lips and stepped out onto the porch to get some fresh air. He shivered, for a drenching mist was being whipped by a cold wind from the north.

"From down the street he heard the beat of a drum and a voice raised in song. He knew that the man responsible for the music was Ensign Olson of the Salvation Army. Olson and his workers frequently sang and played on the street corners in Rogers to obtain contributions for their work and to advertise their nightly meetings. One of the young ladies had caught the eye of the teenager, and a time or so he had held up a few pennies so that she would collect them from him. But that night Olson was alone.

"Down the street he came, his voice and drum getting louder and louder above the howl of the wind and the slosh of the rain. Few Salvation Army officers could sing more lustily or beat a drum with more vigor than he. As he approached the cafe other fellows emerged to make jocular remarks about the Swede singing in the rain. But Olson never paused or missed a note.

"Olson moved on down the street, and the lime kiln gang returned to the warmth and smoke of the little cafe—all but John Elward. He had not laughed or even smiled. As he stood in the cold, damp air he peered up and down the street. There was no one to be seen except Olson and no sound except the beat of Olson's drum.

"But that night the boom, boom, boom of the drum had a power over the young man that he had not felt before. He could not ignore it. He threw away his cigarette, stepped off the cafe porch, and followed Olson and his drum to an upstairs hall over a store building. Brown said to himself, 'If this man is willing to sing and beat his drum on a night like this, he has something I want.'

"For several nights he attended the meetings in the old hall and came under strong conviction. But he hesitated to go forward when the invitation was given for fear that his companions would make fun of him. Finally one night he could wait no longer. He went forward to kneel at the altar and gave his heart to Christ. And he was not alone. Several of his friends, secretly admiring his courage, followed him—perhaps prophetic of the thousands John Brown would lead to Christ in later years.

"In reference to his conversion he said, 'On the night of May 15, I made the decision that has so wonderfully changed my life. I am lost in wonder, and to this day I cannot explain nor do I understand the wonderful workings of God.'

"He knew that Olson had a custom of calling on new converts to give their testimonies on the night following their conversion, and the thought of it was frightening. But he did his best to prepare. He said, 'I studied that speech until I thought l could say it forward or backward, even say it in my sleep; but when the time came for testimonies, I tried to hide behind a large man. When Ensign Olson announced, "We shall now hear from our young friend, Brown," I stood up speechless. I just couldn't talk.' So he stopped under a large tree on the way home and prayed fervently that he might be able to testify in the Sunday morning service.

"That morning the Salvation Army officer called on him to lead in prayer, and Brown said later, 'I prayed like a house afire and could not find a place to stop. The next night I did not wait to be called upon. I was the first to testify. I began talking and have been doing it ever since.'"

Taken from *John Brown of Arkansas* by R. C. Kennedy and T. R. Rothrock. Copyright © 1966, 1977 by JBU Press. Used by permission.

5

WILLIAM JENNINGS BRYAN:
Orator, Crusader, Public Servant

The vast auditorium quickly filled to capacity. The atmosphere seemed tense with expectation as everyone awaited the appearance of the now world-famous William Jennings Bryan, eminent orator, crusader, former member of Congress, three times Democratic candidate for President of the United States. There are not many of us still around who saw and heard "the great commoner" speak, but I was privileged to be among those present on this occasion. None was disappointed, and I for one was deeply impressed, for I still recall the imposing figure, the eloquence, dramatic gestures, and resonant voice.

Among Bryan's most noted speeches was "The Prince of Peace." In an effort to keep our nation out of war, he warned against entanglements which he saw were heading us in that direction and finally in protest resigned as Secretary of State in the cabinet of the President who, seeming not to recognize the danger, made possible our involvement in the fateful first World War.

Traveling through Europe in the summer of 1925, in each large city we came to I would look up an English-edition newspaper—since even in other lands the developments of the famous Scopes evolution trial in Dayton, Tennessee, were being closely followed. The day then arrived when the front-page headline

31

announced the untimely death of William Jennings Bryan. I soon told my father, who had voted for Bryan for President. Bryan's passing was a real loss, for he not only stood for the direct creation of the world and man, but for other great verities of the Christian faith—honesty, sobriety, integrity, and virtue among men, qualities he himself so outstandingly exemplified.

How did this great man come into his Christian experience? The story seems to unfold as follows:

We draw first from *William Jennings Bryan*, by P. E. Coletta. Of Bryan's early years he says, "Both mother and father taught him to obey them and to fear God. From them he learned that he must follow the dictates of the Bible in his temporal as well as in his spiritual life. The prayers the Judge [his father] conducted before the family altar became one of William's 'sweetest recollections.' The Judge was a faithful member of the church and spoke often on religious questions. William, too, became an avid reader and propounder of the Bible and one of the greatest lay leaders of his day.

"William followed his parents in devotion to Protestant evangelistic religion. No theologians, they valued the Bible as the inspired source for salvation and also as a perpetual font for wisdom concerning ethical conduct. The gospel service, the revival, the emphasis upon missions, and the appeal to the heart rather than to the mind in soul-winning—amply sufficed for them. . . . They used the Bible and McGuffey to teach their children the character-forming values of the church, home, and school; the importance of truth, love, obedience, work, and thrift; and the dangers involved in drinking, gambling, dancing, swearing, idleness, and dishonesty. The morality the parents implanted in William made an everlasting impression and hardened as the years went by. He never smoked, gambled, danced, or swore. . . . When about thirteen years old he was hired to help with a threshing. He carried water to the men but refused to bring them whiskey. . . .

"Until he was twelve William attended a Methodist Sunday school in the morning with his mother and a Baptist one in the afternoon with his father, but he was unaware of denominational differences. . . . William and his elder sister made it a practice to attend revival meetings. While in a Presbyterian church they were converted, and they became members."

Perhaps it is more significant to hear Bryan mention these things himself. We turn to *The Memoirs of William Jennings Bryan*, by himself and his wife. For a starter we read, "My religious training was not neglected at any period of my life. We had family prayers—one of the sweetest recollections of my boyhood days—and I entered Sunday school early. My father being a Baptist and my mother being a Methodist, I went to both Sunday schools. . . . At the age of fourteen I reached one of the turning points in my life. I attended a revival that was being conducted in a Presbyterian church and was converted."

It was something that stuck! Many years later, speaking to a body of high school students in Boston, he said, "This audience recalls a day in my life forty-two years ago and more when I was a high school boy, for I was fourteen when I became a member of a Christian church by conversion. I look back to that day as the most important day of my life. It has had far more to do with my life than any other day, and the Book to which I swore allegiance on that day has been more to me then any party platform [many of which he fought for in national conventions]" (*The Life of William Jennings Bryan*, by Herrick and Herrick).

Another gives different sidelights: "Willy's conversion came at the age of fourteen, when Salem's Cumberland Presbyterian Church held a series of revivals. The Cumberland Presbyterians rejected the doctrine that only a select few were predestinated to salvation. . . . He felt equally comfortable in other Protestant churches. Theological distinctions that separated denominations mattered less than personal commitment to Christ and the belief that Christ had a similar commitment to each individual who accepted Him as Savior.

"Silas Bryan [his father] opened his court with prayer, prayed three times each day, led his family in hymn-singing on Sunday afternoons, and brought his children catechisms as presents when he returned from holding court in another county. Young Willy deeply respected his father . . ." (*A Righteous Cause, The Life of William Jennings Bryan*, by R. W. Cherny).

Returning to the *Memoirs* we find Bryan saying, "My father, being a very devout man, lost no opportunity to impress upon me the value of the Bible. To him it was not only the Word of God but the fountain of wisdom. He was especially fond of Proverbs and was in the habit of calling me in from work a little before noon to read me a chapter and comment upon it. I cannot say that I shared his enthusiasm at the time—in fact, I was at times a little restless and even wished that I might have been allowed to devote the time to work in the field rather than to the reading and comment. But when he died, soon after I was twenty, the biblical truths that he sought to impress upon me grew in value, and I took up the book of Proverbs and read it through once a month for a year. I have frequently mentioned this experience and advised young men to read Proverbs."

A word of Bryan's on conversion is interesting. "Conversion, as I understand it, is surrender of one's self to God. . . . And how long does it take to be converted? It takes but an instant for the heart to surrender itself to its Maker and pledge obedience to God" (Herrick and Herrick).

We conclude with these words of Bryan, fitting for our day, "In spite of our intellectual progress and boasted civilization, we are continually compelled to design new laws to protect society from new forms of brutality and crime. There is much of the 'wilderness' even in our crowded cities, and we need the cry of men with souls afire, calling society back to God, to the Bible, and to Christ" (*Illustrations* by Holdcraft).

6

B. H. CARROLL:
Infidel Turned Bible Teacher and Scholar

B H. Carroll never went to a seminary, yet he is credited as the founder and first president of the Southwestern Baptist Theological Seminary (Fort Worth, TX). And not only did he serve in administrative capacities, he taught large classes in Bible, first at Baylor University (Waco, TX), where he became principal of the Bible Department, then as professor at Southwestern. Dr. Carroll was also a voluminous writer whose over 40 books include the 17-volume *An Interpretation of the English Bible*. A great statesman and scholar, the *Wycliffe Biographical Dictionary of the Church* characterizes him as a "powerful preacher, keen debater, ready writer, and a widely-read historian."

We take the story of Dr. Carroll's conversion from a book of his messages (1895), which J. B. Cranfill says in introducing, "It is only when depth of intellect and breadth of attainment are combined with greatness of heart and gentleness of spirit that there is real greatness. Dr. Carroll is, in the highest sense of the term, a genuinely great man. In gifts he towers a very giant among his fellows, while in breadth of learning and research he ranks with the profoundest scholars of the time. But crowning all is his great heart power, his gentleness and humility. . . . He is an omnivorous reader, having averaged 250 pages a day for 35 years."

Carroll's conversion, excerpted from the same volume, follows:

"I cannot remember when I began to be an infidel. Certainly at a very early age. There was nothing in my home life to beget it or suggest it. This skepticism progressed, though the progress was not steady and regular. Thus before I knew what infidelity was, I was an infidel. My child mind was fascinated by strange and sometimes horrible questionings concerning many religious subjects. . . .

"My infidelity related to the Bible and its manifest doctrines. I doubted that it was God's book, that it was an inspired revelation of His will to man. I doubted miracles. I doubted the divinity of Jesus of Nazareth. But more than all, I doubted His vicarious expiation for the sins of men."

When Carroll was thirteen years of age, a revival swept the community where he lived. Great excitement ensued. Many pressed the lad with questions he could not give a negative answer to, so he was told he should be baptized. Thus pressured, he underwent the rite. He says, "I had no confidence in professed conversion—regeneration. I had not felt lost, nor did I feel saved. . . . I felt a repugnance. Honesty required me to say something. And so I merely asked that the church withdraw from me. This was not granted. They asked me to wait and give it a trial, to read the Bible and pray. From that time on I read the Bible and marked its contradictions and fallacies as they seemed to me, from Genesis to Revelation.

"Two years passed away. In this interval we moved to Texas. Now came the period of reading Christian apologies and infidel books. What a multitude of both kinds, Hume, Paine, Voltaire. . . . In the meantime I was in college devouring Greek, Roman, and Oriental philosophies. At seventeen, being worn out in body and mind, I joined McCullough's Texas Rangers."

Carroll came through the Civil War wounded—broken in both body and spirit, capped by experience that left him embittered and lonely. In this state he says, "In the hour of my darkness I turned unreservedly to infidelity. I brought a broken heart and a disappointed life, asking for light and peace and rest. It was now no curious speculation; it was a stricken soul anxiously and earnestly seeking light.

"A dark and deadly warfare raged within me. I do know this: my quest for truth was sincere and unintermittent. With all the earnestness of a soul, I brought a broken but honest heart to every reputed oracle of infidelity. I merely asked light to shine on the path of right. Once more I viewed the anti-Christian philosophies to inquire what they built up, what they offered to a hungry heart and blasted life.

"Why had I never seen it before? How could I have been blind to it? These philosophies, one and all, were mere negations. They were destructive, not constructive. They overturned and overturned and overturned, but as my soul lives, they built up nothing under the whole heaven in the place of what they destroyed. I mean nothing. They looked down on my bleeding heart as the cold, distant, pitiless stars have ever looked down on all human suffering. Whoever in his hour of real need makes abstract philosophy his pillow, makes cold, hard granite his pillow. They are all wells without water and clouds without rain.

"Here now was my case: I had turned my back on Christianity and had found nothing in infidelity; happiness was gone, and death would not come. The Civil War had left me a wounded cripple on crutches, utterly poverty-stricken, loaded with debt. The internal war of infidelity now left me bound like Prometheus on the cold rock, a life that could suffer but could not die. And like Job, I felt the need of a mediator; and like Job, I complained: 'Neither is there any daysman betwixt us, that might lay his hand upon us both.' And thus I approached my twenty-second year.

"I had sworn never to put my foot in another church. My father had died believing me lost. My mother (when does a mother give up a child?) came to me one day and begged, for her sake, that I would attend one more meeting. It was a Methodist camp meeting. I had not an atom of interest in it. I liked the singing, but the preaching did not touch me. But one day I shall never forget. It was Sunday at eleven o'clock. The great wooden shed was crowded. I stood on the outskirts, leaning on my crutches, wearily and somewhat scornfully enduring. There was nothing in the sermon. But when the preacher came down, as I supposed to exhort as usual, he startled me not only by not exhorting, but by asking some questions that seemed meant for me. He said, 'You that stand aloof from Christianity and scorn us simple folks, what have you got? Answer honestly before God; have you found anything worth having where you are?'

My heart answered in a moment, 'Nothing under the whole heaven; absolutely nothing.' As if he had heard my unspoken answer, he continued, 'Is there anything else out there worth trying, that has any promise in it?' Again my heart answered, 'Nothing, absolutely nothing. All these roads lead to a bottomless abyss.' 'Well then,' he continued, 'are you willing to test it? Have you the fairness and courage to try it? To try it now; to make a practical, experimental test; you to be the judge of the results?'

"These cool, calm, and pertinent questions hit me with tremendous force. He continued on the Scripture, 'If any man willeth to do his will, he shall know of the doctrine, whether it be of God.' The preacher quoted it, 'Whosoever willeth to do the will of God,' showing that the knowledge as to whether the doctrine was of God depended not upon external action and not upon exact conformity, but upon internal disposition—'Whosoever willeth to do God's will.' It means that true knowledge follows persistence in the prosecution of it.

"So when he invited all who were willing to make an immediate experimental test to come forward, I immediately went forward. I was not prepared for the stir which this action created. My infidelity and my hostile attitude toward Christianity were so well known in the community that such action on my part developed quite a sensation. Some even began to shout. Whereupon, to prevent any misconception, I arose and stated that I was not converted, that perhaps they misunderstood what was meant by my coming forward; that my heart was as cold as ice; my action meant no more than that I was willing to make an experimental test of the truth and power of the Christian religion, and that I was willing to persist in the test until a true solution could be found. That quieted matters.

"The meeting closed without any change upon my part. I remained to hear a few ladies sing their last song. The singing made a wonderful impression on me. Suddenly there flashed upon my mind, like a light from heaven, this Scripture, 'Come unto me, all ye that labor and are heavy laden, and I will give you rest.' I seemed to see Jesus standing before me, looking reproachfully and tenderly and pleadingly, seeming to rebuke me for having gone to all other sources for rest but the right one, and now inviting me to come to Him. In a moment I went, once and forever, casting myself unreservedly and for all time at Christ's feet, and in a moment the rest came, indescribable and unspeakable, and it has remained from that day until now.

"I gave no public expression of the change which had passed over me but spent the night in the enjoyment of it and wondering if it would be with me when morning came. When the morning came it was still with me, brighter than the sunlight and sweeter than the songs of birds, and now, for the first time, I understood the Scripture which I had often heard my mother repeat, 'Ye shall go out with joy, and be led forth with peace. . . .'"

7

SETON CHURCHILL:
British Soldier and Author

Lieutenant-Colonel Seton Churchill was a British author with a wide and varied experience. I find in the National Union Catalogue (volume 109, 1970), there are eight listings of his published works.

The following story of the many influences which finally led to his assurance of salvation is taken from *Roads to Christ*, edited by C. S. Isaacson.

"Very early in life I selected the Army as a profession, and with that object I was sent to a military 'crammer' at Woolwich. I can never, however, look back on that period without a sense of shame. There was practically no spiritual or even moral influence exerted, and so long as we worked hard to do credit to our instructors, no questions were asked. At that critical age in life when we were budding into manhood, we were allowed to frequent public houses [drinking places], music and dancing saloons, billiard tables and like resorts without the slightest restraint. Even if fellows were not actually immoral, they all pretended to be so, for to be otherwise would not only have made one peculiar but would have been looked upon as a sign that the individual was wanting in manliness. So far as I know, none did suffer the reproach of being peculiar. I have often since wondered at the low standard that it is possible for young fellows of that age to hold among themselves.

"It is recorded of the young man Daniel that his heart was right with God, whereas mine was not. At all events I can lay no flattering unction to my soul that, amid the corrupt surroundings of my early youth, I was any better than the rest with whom I had to associate. I once had a praying mother, but she died when I was very young. I also had an earnest, godly father; I cannot but feel that it is to the prayers of my father and mother that I am indebted for the spiritual change through which I passed.

"When living in the midst of sin, without being any exception to those who were around me, I was startled to hear of the sudden death of a young fellow in the neighborhood of my home. He was older than I and was the type of a fine healthy young Englishman, keenly alive to sport. He was apparently in perfect health and jumped out of a cart to pick up the hat of a friend he was driving, when suddenly he fell dead. I felt his loss most keenly.

"I knew at all events that I was not prepared to meet my God, and this sudden death of one who was stronger and healthier than I enabled me to realize for the first time the uncertainty of life. I ought here to mention that, if I had nothing else in common with that great and good man, the late General Gordon, I had at all events this, that like him I possessed a sister of whom I was very fond, who was a devoted Christian. She it was who wrote me an account of the death of this young fellow; and, with a sister's tact, I expect that she in her quiet way, to use the common expression, rubbed it in well. At all event, from that time I gave up all the open forms of sin and in a feeble way attempted to identify myself with all that was noble, good, and Christ-like.

"Those around me thought that I had 'turned religious,' but I am bound to admit flat at that time I had no peace or happiness. Alas! like too many, I was trying hard to lead a religious life without that living faith which alone is able to give us the victory over the world, the flesh, and the Devil. The results were very unsatisfactory. I had cut myself off from open sin, but, when I came into contact with true Christian people, I was always conscious of the fact that they had something that I had not.

"I passed through the Royal Military College at Sandhurst and was kept from all outward forms of sin at the time when the moral condition of that institution was very bad. Though I became very keen about games and also about my profession, I never had any peace or happiness. I was fond of society and went to dances; but I can distinctly remember feeling in a certain ballroom how unsatisfactory it all was. How many an aching heart, sick of the vanities of this world, is often concealed by a bright exterior! At that time I had everything I could possibly want to make me happy, and which of my many bright companions ever guessed the truth?

"Experiences in the spiritual life vary much. Some I have known have passed through what may be termed 'sudden conversion' similar to that of St. Paul. But such was not my case. Although I had given up the outward forms of sin, I was perfectly ignorant of the most elementary rudiments of religion, and I would gladly have been spoken to about my soul at that time.

"I remember once in the north of Ireland when I was in charge of a company of some detached barracks not far from headquarters, I got an attack of measles. A good clergyman who was acting as chaplain to our troops came to see me. I hoped that he would speak to me about my soul, but he seemed to talk on every topic but the one on which I wanted him to help me, and I was too reserved to take the initiative in opening my heart to him. How any clergyman can conceive that he has done his duty to a sick person by an aimless talk about the weather and other topics equally uninteresting has always since been a mystery to me.

"I was, however, more fortunate later on, for I went to hear an evangelical clergyman, also an Irishman, who had a reputation for being a good preacher. After the service was over, he invited me into his study, and in the course of the conversation, I found how ignorant I was of the most elementary principles of religion. When he spoke to me of a happy assurance to be obtained by simple faith in Christ, it seemed to me as if he was speaking a new language. Here was salvation being offered to me as a free gift. It seemed to me almost too good to be true. Said he, 'I have no other gospel to offer but that offered by St. Paul to the jailer at Philippi, "Believe on the Lord Jesus Christ, and thou shalt be saved."'

"I was quite convinced that night that he was right, but it was some time yet before I could enjoy that peace of mind of which he had been speaking.

"Some time after this, my regiment marched to the garrison

church. A captain of another regiment, after the service was over, introduced himself and asked me if I knew of an officers' Bible-reading to be held that week in the hut of a major of his battalion and invited me to attend it. This was the first time I had ever gone to anything of this kind, and I felt very nervous about it, especially as I remembered that a company of my own regiment which was engaged at musketry at the rifle ranges would be marching home past that particular point at about the same hour.

"Thinking that I was sure to be seen going in and was sure to be chaffed about it at mess that night, I was in a great funk. Oh, what cowards some of us are when we want to do right, but how boldly we will go in for that which is wrong! I was coward enough to be afraid of its being known that I had attended a Bible-reading!

"I remember very well about the Bible-reading, but after it we had some tea, and I got into friendly conversation with a major of a cavalry regiment. After a time he asked me if I was able to realize Christ as my Savior, and I replied that though I was unable to do so, it was the one thing for which I longed. He asked me to come for a walk. Then he took out his Bible and read to me 1 John 5:9–14. This helped me considerably to understand the simple plan of salvation.

"One day I went to call on an officer and found his regiment on parade. As we were old friends, having been cadets at Sandhurst together, I went into his hut to wait till the parade was dismissed. While sitting there thinking that all the officers were on parade and that I was quite alone, I suddenly heard a voice singing, '*O happy day that fixed my choice on Thee, my Savior, and my God! Well may this glowing heart rejoice, and tell its raptures all abroad.*'

"I said to myself, 'That is just what I should like to be able to say.' The words were being sung by an officer, the assistant musketry rope instructor of the regiment who had just returned home from the rifle range. Thinking himself quite alone in the hut, he had given vent to his feelings in these words that came to me like a message from God. Through my friend I got to know him afterward, and he was a great help to us both.

"My bad and unbelieving heart gradually seemed to yield to the constraining power of the Holy Spirit who was all the time ever unconsciously drawing me. Within a very short time I was enabled to say, like one of old, 'But one thing I know, that whereas I was blind, now I see,' and much of that slavish fear of what others would think of me also went.

"More than thirty years have passed away since then, and I have knocked about a good deal in the world, having been twice to India, twice to South Africa, once to Burma, and once to Egypt. During that long period I have made many mistakes in life, but looking back over the past I have never regretted that step taken when I was quite a young subaltern. It is the one bright spot that shines out in relief against a dark background of failings and shortcomings on my part."

8

CAPTAIN ALLEN GARDINER:
British Naval Captain and Missionary Martyr

Captain Allen Gardiner rose rapidly in the British Royal Navy, serving in various parts of the world, and fought against us in the War of 1812 in which he distinguished himself in the capture of the American frigate *Essex*.

While Gardiner's life was characterized throughout by a spirit of adventure, after his conversion this apparent restlessness was marked by a sincere desire to spread the gospel of Christ to one after another of the unreached parts of the earth. In *Progress of World-Wide Missions*, Robert Hall Glover says, "This noble British naval officer had seen service in many parts of the world, was converted during one of his voyages, and became filled with a passion for Christ and lost souls."

Indeed, Gardiner was seen, before his tragic and untimely death, at one time in Newfoundland, then India, then laboring for Christ in the Zulu country of Africa, then Bolivia, New Guinea and the East Indies, Australia, Patagonia, Chile, the Falkland Islands, and elsewhere. Entailing great hardship and suffering in that early day, he took his family by wagon across the Andes. Arthur T. Pierson said (*The New Acts of the Apostles*), "Allen Gardiner was an enthusiast, a fanatic, but in the eyes of God he was fired with a divine passion."

The story of Gardiner's conversion can be found in his biographies; one we have by Marsh and Stirling, another by Jesse Page.

Gardiner had the advantage of being born into a godly home. "Their regular observance of family prayer was never forgotten by their illustrious son" (Page).

After the capture of the American ship in the War of 1812, where "both vessels had suffered severely," Gardiner was "put on board the *Prize*, and, after some difficulty, she and her captive [American] crew were brought safely to Portsmouth." We read on, "At this time, however, he had already drifted into that reckless career which was the life his worldly companions led. The thought of God seemed to have faded from his mind, and only at times of great peril and hazard did he seem to welcome the consideration of eternal things. Several narrow escapes showed him how near the borders of the unseen land his calling led him. While off the coast of Peru the boat in which he was going ashore suddenly capsized, and he only just saved his life by swimming. Very soon afterward a similar accident occurred again, but this time a young midshipman comrade was drowned before his eyes. Still, the solemn thoughts engendered by these sad events soon passed away."

After the death of his devoted mother, we read further, "Allen lost interest and mingled still more freely in the revels and godlessness of his companions. More than that, he began to imbibe infidel opinions, and the glorious truths upon which he had been nourished as a boy became an object of mocking ridicule and scorn. He was fast drifting, and to those who knew him at this period of his life there seemed to be no probability of his becoming a true and faithful witness for Christ.

"One day when at Portsmouth, he was walking the streets with many serious unusual thoughts. The loss of a friend by sudden death had made him grave, and he determined to purchase a Bible. It was a long time since he had read the Scriptures, and when he came to a bookseller's shop, he walked up and down the street half ashamed to make his purchase. When he found an opportunity unobserved, he went in and bought his Bible. The perusal of this little volume, although his conversion did not immediately follow, prepared the way for that great decision. Once more he set sail with a squadron of warships for India, whence after a short stay, his ship moved on to China.

"When Gardiner was at Penang [western Malaya], letters came from England, one from his father and the other from a lady who had taken a very deep interest in him from the time that, as a cadet, he came into the Naval College. This lady had been his sincere friend and had watched with much regret the waywardness of his life in later years. Her conversations had not been lost upon him, and she had put in his hand a record of the last few months preceding his mother's death.

"It was at this crisis of his life, with the deep impressions made by this letter fresh upon his mind, that Gardiner, shortly afterward sailing to the coast of South America, made acquaintance with Christianity in mixed and superstitious worship. Walking through the streets of Santiago, he saw in the cathedral of that city the gaudy magnificence of its ritual, and afterward, when visiting one of the monasteries in the neighborhood, was struck with the levity of the monks, and how little the priests cared. . . .

"His vessel was returning to China when it was found necessary to call at Tahiti on its way. It so happened that the ship reached the island on a Sunday morning, and Gardiner at once noticed that an atmosphere of peace pervaded the place. . . . Christian work among these natives had not long been established, but the teaching of the missionaries had already transformed the people, and when he entered their place of worship, he was struck with the thoughtfulness and decorum of the congregation."

Later, "Calling at Cape Town, he recalls his feelings on his last visit, and there is evidence in the entries he makes in his journal that a great change had taken place in his heart and life."

We now quote from his journal his own woe regarding the change wrought (as in Marsh and Stirling), "The last time I visited this colony [Cape Town] I was walking in the broad way and hastening by rapid strides to the brink of eternal ruin. Blessed be His name who loved us and gave Himself for us; a great change has been wrought in my heart, and I am now enabled to derive pleasure and satisfaction in reading the Word of God. I trust that this alteration has, indeed, been effected by the Spirit of God. . . .

"Alas, how slow, how reluctant have I been to admit the heavenly Guest who stood knocking without! Too frequently am I ashamed to acknowledge the Hand that was stretched out for my relief, to own the Word that warned me on the brink of ruin, or to be seen supplicating that assistance by which alone I can be prevented from stumbling over the dreadful abyss."

The rest of the story was marked by sacrificial endeavors to extend the knowledge of that saving grace. Indeed, a mission to the Zulus of east Africa was undertaken with energy, though short-lived due to unfortunate wars and politics. Earlier, when establishing the port of Natal in that region, he was instrumental in founding the city to which he gave the name Durban in honor of Sir Benjamin Durban, governor of the Cape.

Gardiner's final and most famous mission was to the land of wild climate and wilder tribes, the far southern end of South America. We read in Glover, "The Indians of that extreme southern tip of the continent and the adjacent Island of Tierra del Fuego were among the most degraded people in the world. The eminent naturalist, Charles Darwin, dubbed them 'the missing link' between man and monkey and declared them incapable of moral discernment. Gardiner accepted this challenge and was permitted to labor long enough to convince Darwin of his error."

The end of the story is quickly told. After earlier attempts to establish a mission in these parts, Gardiner returned to England, organized a new society, and with six other capable and brave men, landed on Tierra del Fuego. The savages denied them any succor, stole from them unashamedly, and drove them away from any site suitable for a settlement. Known to have only six months of supplies, a relief shipment was promised but never arrived. Just as British forces promised to lift the siege of General Gordon at Khartoum were slow in arriving and the object of their intended rescue perished, so in the case of Gardiner the promised relief failed them.

Dr. Glover (himself of British background) graphically depicts it, "Driven from their center at Banner Cove by the truculence and pilfering of the unregenerate Indians, Gardiner and six companions from England put to sea in their little vessel and took refuge in Spanish Harbor, where they waited and prayed for the coming of the promised supply ship from home. Before it arrived starvation had slowly overtaken every member of the heroic little band, Gardiner himself being the last to succumb. Their bodies and diaries were found to tell the pathetic tale. . . . The news stirred the Church of England to its depths and gave new impulse to the work among the Indians."

Arthur T. Pierson records, "Such was his passionate love for God that, even while starving, he could record nothing save marvels of mercy. Over the place where he lay down to die he had inscribed on the rock, 'My soul, wait thou only upon God, for my expectation is from Him' (Psalm 62:5). Men who read or heard this pathetic tale knew not which emotion was mightier, horror at such a tale of suffering, or admiration at such dauntless heroism."

But all was not in vain; fruit sprang forth. The eminent authority on missions, Dr. Robert E. Speer, said, "The first enduring Protestant Mission to South America began with the sacrifice of Captain Allen Gardiner who perished of starvation in Tierra del Fuego" (quoted in Glover). Pierson said, "He had sown in tears, but today among heathen tribes there is springing up a plenteous harvest. Faith was tried but triumphed."

9

OLIVER B. GREENE:
Tent Preacher and Radio Evangelist

Oliver B. Greene was a tent preacher for 25 years, one of the best known fundamentalist evangelists in the Southeast, and a radio broadcaster heard on a nationwide network. In tent meetings alone over two hundred thousand professions of faith were recorded, and he preached over nine thousand times on the radio. All of his ministries were by faith and without sponsors or underwriters, including the publishing ministry which printed and sent out one million booklets during a twenty-year period.

The story of his life and ministry is graphically told in his *From Disgrace to Grace*. Most of the following is excerpted from it in his own words.

"I made friends with bad boys. I took up all the bad habits. Young as I was, I had acquired the habit of smoking. I did not have the money to buy cigarettes, so I stole them out of my Dad's little country store. . . . In that store he lost all that he had ever made. I furnished all the bad boys with cigarettes at Dad's expense.

"When I was only nine years old I took my first drink, but it was by no means my last. I loved the stuff from the very first drink. I went from bad to worse. I was known as the lad who could pour moonshine from a half-gallon jar into a pint bottle in the moonlight and never spill a drop. And I could actually do that. . . .

"The next bad step I took was stealing Dad's money. He would lock it up, but I would make a key to fit the lock. He would hide it, but I would find it. God only knows how much of my poor Dad's money I stole and ran through with it. I continued to drink more and more. Nothing that happened seemed to help me. I would have close calls, and they would shake me up for a while, but then I would go right back to the same old gang and the same old life. I drank, gambled, ran around like a dog, and paid no attention to God's warnings. Sin was wrapping its cords tighter and tighter around my poor soul.

"The devil had me and I knew it. I was ungodly. I was not fit to live, but God loved me. All that I cared for was liquor and a big time. I do not believe there is another poor soul alive today who has gotten by with so much, committed so much sin, so many crimes, and yet escaped the penitentiary. I stole anything I could get my hands on, and from anybody. I broke into two different places of business and stole goods. I would even steal gasoline from cars at church and hide it under the church until everybody had gone, and then I would go back and get it. But I have been to all from whom I stole and have made it all right since I was saved.

"I had almost killed my poor parents with my riotous living. I had stolen so much of Dad's money that as a result he lost his farm and his business. He died on a mortgaged farm—partly because of my riotous living. I stooped to the lowest level."

Greene tells how he came home night after night, sometimes after 2:00 A.M., to find his mother up and praying, pleading with tears for her boy. When he was sick as an infant, his mother had prayed for God to spare his life. Now she regretted these prayers and asked God to take him or save him from worse things.

"Thank God, in spite of my vile living I had a sister who loved me, and who night after night prayed for me. She prayed for ten long years. God finally answered her prayers and saved her wretched brother.

"It was not long after I had moved down into the country with my Dad that I met a fine, clean, country girl. I fell in love with the young lady in just a few short weeks. She had a lot of influence on me. She did not smoke, drink, or curse—and that had its influence on my life. I did not drink around her; I did not curse in her presence unless I became awfully mad at someone, and then I would let fly!

"Shortly after falling in love with this young woman, one Sunday night I wanted Dad's automobile to take her to the lake in the community. The weather was still warm enough to go swimming. But I ran into trouble. There was a revival meeting in the little town about ten miles from where we lived. My sister wanted to go to the revival, but the only way she had to go was for me to drive her, since she herself could not drive. There was only one car in the family, and I was the only one who could drive it; therefore, unless I drove the car, she would be unable to attend church. I did not want to take her to church, but Dad informed me that if I did not take her to the revival, I would not be allowed to use the car that night. I cussed for ten minutes and finally said, 'Okay, I'll take her.' But I did it only because I was forced to.

"I took my poor embarrassed sister and went by for my girl friend. We then went to the church where the revival was in progress. Before I knew it I was being dragged down the church aisle. When I came to myself, I was sitting within five feet of the altar. If there had been a crack in the floor, I would have gone to the basement through that crack! I was in total misery.

"The pastor of the church came to the platform and announced a certain hymn. Then three young ladies came to the platform to sing. These three girls were not beautiful; they were not even what you would call attractive girls. They were not wearing make-up like other girls, but I have never seen such beaming, happy faces in all my life. I did not know at that time what made their faces glow so brightly, but I know now. They were filled with the love of God and the Spirit of God. They were there to sing because they loved Jesus. They opened their part of the program by singing a little chorus, 'Isn't It Grand to Be a Christian?' Those girls proved to me that it was grand *for them* to be Christian. I wondered if they could really be that happy. Every song they sang had the same joyful ring. Their voices sounded out His praise so fervently I knew it had to be genuine. I was amazed. I found myself wishing they would sing more. I could not tell you the subject of the preacher's message that night. But those beaming faces and those words, 'Isn't it grand to be a Christian?' continued to ring in my ears. I could not get them out of my mind.

"This was on the last night of the meeting. I took my sister home. I took my girl home. As a rule I sat in the car and talked with her for an hour or so after we came home, but on this particular night I did not want to talk with anyone. I went to the door with her and told her goodnight.

"All the next week I lived in a daze. I played jazz and hillbilly music, but now the only words and music I could hear were, 'Isn't it grand to be a Christian?' I must have acted like one who was losing his mind. Mother watched me continually. I suppose she thought I would attempt suicide again. I did not go anywhere at night, which was very unusual for me. I was most miserable.

"The next Sunday a revival was in progress (at another church). The young minister who was doing the preaching was really a ball of fire. My sister wanted to hear him, and I knew that if I got my Dad's car for the night, I would first have to take her to the revival. Deep down in my heart I wanted to go but was ashamed to admit it. However, if it had not been for my sister's going, I would not have gone; I only went because I had to take her.

"I stood in the door with some other men and listened to the singing. When the singing was over, the young minister came to the pulpit with a spring in his step, a broad smile on his face, and a determination in his eyes. He had captured the attention of his people, so he fired away. 'I am speaking tonight from Romans 6:23,' he announced. 'My subject: *The wages of sin is death.*'" That young man fired words at his audience, words of warning, words which cut like a sharp two-edged sword. And that is what he was preaching—the Word of God!

"As I stood in the door of that little country church, I found myself drinking in every word the man was saying. Instead of being cynical and making fun in my heart, I found myself feeling peculiarly queer inside. There was a lump in my throat; I was forced to admit that the preacher's message had done something to me. At other times I would have walked away from that door, smoked a cigarette, and laughed the whole thing off. But my feet would not move; I could not walk away. I felt a strong fear gripping my soul, and I realized that I was a terrible sinner. I knew I deserved to go to hell after I had treated my parents as I had and after I had treated God as I had, even to the extent of cursing Him.

"I found myself trembling when the preacher said, 'Are you prepared to meet God?' I drank in every word. 'And now in closing,' the preacher said, 'I want you to bow your head and ask yourself this question: "If I should die tonight, where would I spend eternity?" If you are not ready to meet God, then lift your hand and let me pray for you.'

"I wanted so much to lift my hand for prayer, but I did not. It seemed that I could not. The preacher began to pray. He prayed for all those who had raised their hands, and then he prayed for that dear soul who wanted to lift his hand but whom the devil prevented from doing so. I knew he was praying for me.

"When the preacher had finished his prayer, he said, 'Let us all stand and sing. Come forward for prayer. Even though you did not raise your hand, come.' Several went forward for prayer, and I wanted to but did not. They sang three stanzas. Then the preacher said that the next stanza would close the invitation. My heart began to beat faster and faster. I felt cold chills, and I just could not stand there any longer. So I found myself walking toward the preacher. This was something I never dreamed I would ever do. I went forward and gave the preacher my hand and asked him to pray for me. He tried to persuade me to stay for prayer, but I would not. I went back to the door and stood where I had been standing during the service.

"The preacher dismissed the service, and I walked away from that church door with a heavy, sin-sick heart. I waited near the door for my girl friend, and when she came out we went to the car and sat down. I did not say one word. I know she wondered what on earth had happened to me, but I did not care.

"My sister finally came to the car. I started the motor, put the car in gear to start for home, but I could not do so. I cut the motor off and without a word got out and went back into the church. Everyone except the preacher had already gone. I walked through the door and started down the aisle. When the preacher saw me he came to meet me. I am sure he could tell by looking into my face that I was deeply burdened and under conviction. 'What is your trouble?' he asked in a kind, tender voice. 'I'm lost and on the road to hell,' was my reply. He reached into his pocket and took out a little Testament, opened it, and began to read John 3:16. He read very slowly, emphasizing the words. When he had finished he looked directly into my face and said, 'Do you believe that?' He explained to me that I must believe *on* Jesus, that I must trust Him as the Savior of my soul, and that I must accept Him as my personal Savior, just as I would receive a gift.

"And then he gripped my hand in his, looked me straight in the eyes, and said, 'With all your heart will you simply say, "Jesus I want You for my Savior; I want You to come into my heart and forgive my sins and save my soul; save me Jesus through Your shed blood."' I looked at him with tears in my eyes and said, 'Preacher, the very best I know how I will do just that.' And I did just that! I bowed my head with him, and he prayed for me. With all my heart I did all that I knew to do, and the Lord understood—*He saved me that moment!*

"I went back to the car, and without one word I started the motor and turned the automobile toward home. I was weeping, and my girl friend and my sister surely understood, for they did not say one word."

10

DOROTHY HASKIN:
From Cult Follower to Christian Writer

D orothy C. Haskin has been writing for Christian magazines and producing books for well nigh forty years. She has also conducted Christian writers' classes. Her books have been published in six different languages. And she has been vitally interested in missions, serving important roles in their promotion. She spent over eight months in the Orient visiting missionaries, which gave her rich material for her writing. Other travels have included Europe, Central America, Equador, and other lands.

The story of her conversion follows, taken from a leaflet by Miss Haskin entitled "I Was a Heathen."

"Though I grew up in the United States, I was as much a heathen as any savage in darkest Africa. My mother's parents had been Protestant, and after my parents' divorce, my mother was attracted by the promises of the cults which flourish in so-called Christian America.

"My earliest religious memory is walking down the street, when I was about eight years old, repeating the 'Scientific Statement of Being.' When other children were learning the Lord's Prayer and the

Twenty-Third Psalm, I was taught, 'There is no life, truth, intelligence nor substance in matter. All is infinite Mind. . . . Matter is mortal error. Spirit is the real and eternal; matter is the unreal and temporal . . .' (*Science and Health with Key to the Scriptures*, by Mary Baker Eddy, p. 468).

"I repeated these sentences because I was afraid of Animal Magnetism. Mother sent me to the Christian Science Sunday School, and though the teachers taught the nothingness of matter, they also taught that it could hurt me unless I repeated the Scientific Statement of Being often enough. I used to walk down the street while repeating it over and over so no automobile nor disease germ could hurt me. I was taught to trust the repeating of it the same as a savage chants a meaningless phrase over and over again to ward off evil spirits.

"Mother went from Christian Science to Unity, to Theosophy, to Numerology, to Astrology, with a dash of Palmistry, Reincarnation and finally Spiritualism.

"Theosophy and related metaphysics absorbed her for many years, making her a morbid, brooding, unhappy woman. I reflected her state of mind, becoming in my late teens a depressed, fear-bound girl. . . .

"I think Astrology was the worst. For years mother lived by her chart. If the day were an ill-omened day on the chart, she would not even use the telephone nor bake a cake. She would remain in bed writing letters or reading more metaphysics. We would keep the house dark, and I usually read a dramatic novel, for though her beliefs overshadowed my life, making it a dark and mystic thing, I was too young to spend the day struggling through the mental calisthenics of these cults. Every detail of my life was bound by superstition. Fear was my constant companion.

"Mother's one sign of good luck was when her left hand itched. It meant we would receive money. Perhaps I would get work, or she would, or we would receive some of the ever overdue alimony. I used to think I would be really grown-up when my own hand would itch, and I could foretell good luck. I waited vainly for that day. My hand never seemed to itch at the right time. Mother told me that the power would not pass to me until her death.

"Spiritualism was Mother's last cult. The first time Mother and I went to a meeting, the medium said my grandmother wanted to contact us and that she carried a birdcage in her hand. This completely captivated my mother because my grandmother's name had been Bird. Surely it was the Devil's delusion. After that, Mother poured out money for private sittings. We used to go to the medium's home, to the darkness of the cellar, and with others sit around a table singing my grandmother's favorite hymn. But Grandmother never materialized.

"How long ago that all seems! After vainly searching, believing their false claims without results, when forty-seven, Mother in desperation shot herself. She had found nothing in life to satisfy her. The shock of her death sent me searching. I paid a Christian Scientist practitioner to tell me that my mother had become part of the Infinite. I paid a spiritualist medium to tell me Mother would wander in outer darkness until the time came when she would have died naturally. A Catholic priest suggested that I pray her out of purgatory.

"Finally, weary, I telephoned a nearby church and, unwilling to hear the minister preach, I asked if they had a weekday Bible class. They had. I attended it and was surprised to learn that just because one is born, one is not a child of God. 'But as many as received Him, to them gave He power to become the sons of God, even to them that believe on His name' (John 1:12).

"My next question was, believe what? That 'All have sinned, and come short of the glory of God' (Romans 3:23). It was not hard to search my heart and find sin there, but what should I do with it? I found the answer in, 'That if thou shalt confess with thy mouth the Lord Jesus, and shalt believe in thine heart that God hath raised Him from the dead, thou shalt be saved' (Romans 10:9).

"Yes, in Christ I was saved, not only from sin, but in Him I found the answer to *all* my fears and questions. I became a new creature in Christ Jesus. Since then I have faced the false teachings of the cults in the light of Christ and God's Word. Christ alone is the answer.

"I thank Christ for freeing me from the mumbo-jumbo of heathen cults. It is a relief to get up in the morning and know that the letters in my name, the stars, animal magnetism, and not even the lines on my hands can affect me because, 'If the Son therefore shall make you free, ye shall be free indeed' (John 8:36)."

11

ADONIRAM JUDSON:
America's Preeminent Missionary

Adoniram Judson is considered the first, and by some authorities the greatest missionary to go from this continent. Dr. George Smith calls him "the greatest of all American missionaries," saying, "Adoniram Judson is surpassed by no missionary since the apostle Paul in devotion and scholarship, in labors and perils, in saintliness and humility, in the result of his toils. . . ." Judson and his companions formed the first foreign mission board in America.

Judson and his young bride sailed for India. But as R. H. Glover (himself of British background) says, Judson "arrived in Calcutta only to be ordered out by the despotic and gospel-hating East India Company." Determined to press on, they took ship for Burma. Being adept in languages, Judson soon mastered the Burmese language. "But these results were not achieved without the keenest suffering in addition to arduous toil. When war broke out in 1824 between Burma and England, Judson, suspected of being a spy, was thrown into prison."

A. C. Bowers describes it as "terrible months kept tied and chained, hand and foot, in a filthy jail that crawled with vermin, and where the night was crazy with the deep hum of tens of thousands of stinging mosquitoes. While the burning fire of malaria drove him almost insane, the disgusting filth of his surroundings tortured his soul."

And where was Mrs. Judson during this time? J. A. Graham well describes her part. "The heroic Mrs. Judson, though free, suffered quite as much. Sowing the seeds of an early death, she followed her husband 'from prison to prison, ministering to his wants, trying to soften the hearts of his keepers to mitigate his sufferings, interceding with government officials or with members of the royal family. For a year and a half she thus exerted herself, walking miles in feeble health, in darkness of the night or under a noonday sun, much of the time with a babe in her arms.'" Adding to their grief, the babe did not survive.

The story has often been told how she pled with the jailers to allow him to have a stiff pillow she had prepared for him, in which she had secreted the precious manuscript of his translation of the New Testament he had worked so hard on. It was thrown away but in the providence of God rescued by a sympathetic national.

The actual story of his conversion, the key to all, is intensely interesting.

Young Judson had both an active mind and an adventurous spirit. We take the story from *Judson of Burma* by Alfred Mathieson. It seems that Adoniram's younger sister was his confidante, and much was later recounted by her. As the young man pondered life's possibilities, she reports, "He always said and thought, so far as he had thought anything about it, that he wished to become truly religious; but now religion seemed so entirely opposed to all his ambitious plans, that he was afraid to look into his heart lest he should discover what he did not like to confess—even to himself—that he did not want to become a Christian."

Judson entered what is now Brown University, Providence, Rhode Island. His brilliance was recognized, and he became valedictorian of his class. But, as Mathieson points out, "The seeds of infidelity, the production of the French Revolution, had been wafted across the ocean and scattered throughout the land, producing their evil crop of tares.

"An amiable, talented, witty young man, by the name of E_____, in the class above young Judson had imbibed these ideas, and between the young men a very strong friendship sprang up. During the days they were together, the infidel notions came up for discussion. The influence of this fascinating personality had its evil effects upon the youth, so far safeguarded from infidel ideas, and resulted in young Judson becoming, or at least professedly so, as great an unbeliever as his friend."

After graduation Judson opened a private school and even published two textbooks, one on English grammar and one on arithmetic! But before long he closed the school, deciding to venture forth in the exciting world around him. Much to his parents' grief, his adventurous travels began.

The narrative of his sister takes up the story. "One night he stopped at a country inn. The landlord mentioned, as he lighted him to his room, that he had been obliged to place him next door to a young man who was exceedingly ill, probably in a dying state, but he hoped it would occasion him no uneasiness. Judson assured him that, beyond pity for the poor sick man, he should have no feeling whatever, and that now having heard of the circumstance, his pity would not of course be increased by the nearness of the object.

"But it was, nevertheless, a very restless night. Sounds came from the sick chamber—sometimes the movements of the sufferer, but it was not these which disturbed him. He thought of what the landlord had said—the stranger was probably in a dying state; and was he prepared? Alone, and in the dead of night, he felt a blush of shame steal over him at the question, for it proved the shallowness of his philosophy. What would his late companions say to his weakness? The clear-minded, intellectual, witty E____, what would he say to such consummate boyishness?

"But still his thoughts would revert to the sick man. Was he a Christian, calm and strong in the hope of a glorious immortality? Or was he shuddering upon the brink of a dark, unknown future? Perhaps he was a 'freethinker,' educated by Christian parents and prayed over by a Christian mother. The landlord had described him as a young man, and in imagination he was forced to place himself upon the dying bed, though he strove with all his might against it.

"At last morning came, and the bright flood of light which it poured into his chamber dispelled all his 'superstitious illusions.' As soon as he had risen, he went in search of the landlord and inquired for his fellow-lodger. 'He is dead,' was the reply. 'Dead!' 'Yes, he is gone, poor fellow! The doctor said he would probably not survive the night.' 'Do you know who he was?' 'O yes, it was a young man from Providence College [later Brown University]—a very fine fellow; his name was E_____.'

"Judson was completely stunned. After hours had passed he knew not how, he attempted to pursue his journey. But one single thought occupied his mind, and the words, 'Dead! lost! lost!' were continually ringing in his ears. . . . He was in despair. In this state of mind he resolved to abandon his scheme of traveling and at once turned his horse's head toward Plymouth (home)."

Mathieson observes, "The circumstances of this tragic event burned its impression on his soul, but as yet there was no yielding to God. The conflict with doubt still raged. He was like a ship tossed upon the sea."

Finding it hard to know what to do, upon repeated urging, Judson consented somewhat reluctantly to enter the recently formed Andover Theological Seminary, but only as a special student. Mathieson takes up the story, "As he was not a professing Christian, he was admitted only by special favor. He commenced the studies of the second year, and to do so shows his proficiency in the languages of the Old and New Testaments.

"At this time he had not found forgiveness through Christ. He had become thoroughly dissatisfied with the views which he had formerly cherished and was convinced of his sinfulness and his need of a great moral transformation. Yet he doubted the authenticity of revealed religion and clung to the deistical ideas which he had lately imbibed. . . .

"The professors of the seminary encouraged his residence there, wisely judging that so diligent an inquirer must soon arrive at the truth. The result justified their anticipations. In the calm retirement of Andover, guided in his studies by men of learning and piety with nothing to distract his attention from the great concerns of eternity, light gradually dawned upon his mind, and he was enabled to surrender his whole soul to Christ as his atoning Savior. In May 1809, he made a public confession of Christ and joined the church.

"The change wrought in Mr. Judson was deep and real. With simplicity of purpose he yielded himself up once and forever to the will of God and, without a shadow of misgiving, relied upon Christ as his all-sufficient Savior. The new creation was manifest to his consciousness. His plan of life was, of course, entirely reversed."

The rest of the story is familiar. Amid great hardships in Burma, including being stunned by the successive loss of two wives and several children, he nevertheless lived to complete both a grammar and dictionary of the difficult Burmese language and the translation of the whole Bible into Burmese. Broken in health, however, he sought relief in a sea voyage, but dying very shortly thereafter, he was buried at sea.

12

DR. HOWARD A. KELLY:
Surgeon, Scientist, Man of Faith

During the twenties, thirties, and beyond, when doubts about the Bible were being freely expressed on every hand (or so it seemed), the testimony of Dr. Howard A. Kelly stood out most forcefully. The years referred to included my own college days when, confronted by secular educational trends, I was beset by questions as to whether the truly scientific mind could embrace the old-time faith. Then attention was drawn to the case of a world-renowned man of scientific bent who proved by personal experience that the Christian faith could stand in a world of contrary winds.

What are Dr. Kelly's credentials?

The editor of *Appleton's Magazine* long ago said, "Dr. Howard Kelly of Baltimore holds a position almost unique in his profession. With academic, professional, and honorary degrees from the Universities of Pennsylvania, Washington and Lee, Aberdeen, and Edinburgh, his rank as a scholar is clearly recognized. Professor of obstetrics and gynecology at Johns Hopkins University, his place as a worker and teacher in the applied science of his profession has been beyond question the highest in America and Europe. At least a dozen learned societies in England, Scotland, Ireland, Italy, Germany, Austria, France, and the United States have welcomed him to membership as a master in his specialty—surgery. Finally, his published works have caused him to be reckoned the most eminent of all authorities in his own field."

Years later *Time* magazine reported in a three-column article, with a full column photo of the subject, "Dr. Howard A. Kelly, famed Baltimore surgeon, gynecologist, and roentgenologist, having passed 74 [is] about to round out his 50th year in the practice of medicine. . . . Dr. Kelly has two great prides—exactness and versatility. . . . Besides several books, he has written about 500 technical papers having to do with gynecology and other abdominal subjects. His latest work published: *Electrosurgery.* . . . Apart from his medical work, he is a naturalist of repute. A favorite apothegm: 'I love to study nature because I find on all her open pages the signature of the Creator, my Father.' . . . He once took a five-foot gray and yellow king snake before a Congressional Committee to startle them into approving the creation of Everglades National Park at the southwest tip of Florida. The king snake was his library pet."

Dr. Kelly's testimony gives much attention to what established his own firm convictions regarding the Bible and the Christian faith, and it becomes evident that the solid position of assurance he arrived at sprang from a personal, soul-transforming experience which the thoughtful reader can discern throughout.

For the main portion of Dr. Kelly's story we go to an interview he granted which was published in *The American Magazine* (the Crowell Publishing Co., 1924). It is introduced by a statement which we take to be from the editor of that magazine, "Dr. Howard A. Kelly, world-famous surgeon and scientist, says the religion of the Bible made him, literally, another man, and he tells how it has remade other men—an extraordinary story, coming from a great heart and a great mind."

The interviewer, a Mr. William S. Dutton, begins by saying of Dr. Kelly, "He is one of the world's greatest surgeons and gynecologists, an authority on radium, a naturalist known for his interest in fungi and reptilia, an author of wide note in the medical and scientific world, an accomplished linguist and traveler," etc. "I listened with amazement, for I had come to think of great scientists as strongly inclined to skepticism. . . . Dr. Kelly left no room for any misunderstanding. He was most explicit and made it clear that his faith is not a matter of blind inheritance." The interview followed, of which we give but highlights.

"Why am I a Christian?" Dr. Kelly repeated, continuing, "Let's begin at the beginning. As far back as I have any memories, the claims of the Christian faith have been vital in my thought. My mother was the most devout Christian I have ever known. When I was three years old, she began teaching me Bible verses. The Civil War was on, and father was away at the front. Doubtless, the seriousness of the time and my mother's sincere faith registered upon me, small as I was, and left indelible memories. . . . The Bible in our home was not a book of records of births and marriages. It was in constant use. Mother not only asserted its value, but she convinced us of it by her own life and her use of it.

"In later years with wider contacts with the world, I often met men who scoffed at the Bible. While at college, my associates were afraid it would take all the pleasure out of life by checking natural impulses. I realized, however, from God's living Word and from experience, that Christianity was preeminently adapted to our human needs and that it was a workable proposition. . . .

"After all, not even in evidences, welcome as they are, does faith find her resting place, but in the Person of Christ. *Experto credite* (believe one who knows by experience) is a good old motto. I have tried it, and I know it is true."

Dr. Kelly then said he was struck with the wording of John 7:17, "If any man will to do his will, he shall know of the doctrine, whether it be of God. . . .'" "'Why,' I exclaimed, 'that's a challenge! Clear enough in English, even more forceful in the original Greek where the word . . . is "desirous of doing" His will. It is a challenge to stop speculations and prove the doctrine by putting it in one's own life! Surely nothing could be more scientific and reasonable. Indeed, all science is built upon just that experimental basis. I accepted this gracious challenge,' Dr. Kelly went on simply, 'in a new sense about thirty-three years ago.'

"'Now the Bible does work, and it does just what it promises to do—transforms life and brings into it new interests and new affections, making it, through Christ, God-centered. The love of God, shed abroad in the heart by Christ's Holy Spirit, both confers new interests and establishes new standards of right and wrong. . . . Such a change, in the Word of God, is called a "new birth," and it is just as literally a spiritual birth as was the first birth in the flesh. The Christian life is simply the response of the affections to a great love manifested in Christ's death upon the cross, opening up the way of approach to God.'

"Is it literally true," I asked, "that Christianity remakes men?"

"'Yes, belief in the Bible gives new affection, new eyes, new tastes and interests, new expectations and desires. It throws a man's horizon far out beyond the grave and into eternity.'"

From another source we cite this: Dr. Kelly declares, "I believe the Bible to be God's Word because as I use it as spiritual food I discover in my own life, as well as in the lives of those who likewise use it, a transformation, correcting evil tendencies, purifying affections. It reveals to me, as no other book in the world could do, that which appeals to me as a physician, a diagnosis of my spiritual condition. It shows me clearly what I am by nature—one lost in sin. It also reveals a tenderness and nearness of God in Christ which satisfies the heart's longings. And it is intellectual suicide, knowing it, not to believe it."

Continuing the interview with Dr. Howard A. Kelly which we cited last, taken from *The American Magazine*, the world renowned scientist backed up what he said with the following (given just as Dr. Kelly told it):

"You ask for some dramatic, sudden change in men's lives. Let me cite two instances which have come under my observation in Philadelphia. I want to tell you of two men whom Christianity built anew—not reformed but transformed, as the alchemist would try to turn the baser metals into gold. These are not their names, but let us call them Wallace and MacLellan. They were originally chums in their native Scotland, where Wallace married, while MacLellan remained single. Together, thirty-odd years ago, they came to America as textile workers.

"They settled in the old mill district of Kensington, in Philadelphia, where my sister, Mrs. Bradford [like her brother, an outstanding Christian], was just beginning her work. Both were drinking men, a habit brought with them from the old country, so they drifted naturally into the saloons of the mill district. They were hale and likable young fellows, capable of a good song or a tough story.

"Wallace, the stronger of the two, was the leader. He was an intelligent man, industrious and capable in his trade, born as he was of sturdy Scotch stock. But in time he began to slip down the ladder, while MacLellan slipped lower. Wallace's wife also became a drunkard, and he served time in jail. The two men became steeped in sin, and they laughed at all talk of God.

"My sister knew both of them but had more frequent opportunities of seeing Wallace at his home, where he had two attractive children who, because of their father's life, had to live in a wretched dwelling and in evil surroundings. Time after time Wallace, with a shrug and a growingly bitter laugh, rebuffed my sister's effort to serve them.

"One day, meeting her on the street, he told her in a tone of challenge where he had at last come to live. The house was in such a notoriously evil quarter that he believed she would not care to go there.

"But she went. Wallace's house consisted of three rooms, built one over the other and connected by a stairway. He was there, and he let her into the first-floor room. He and his wife were both barefooted, and the children were in rags and half starved. Upstairs were some half-drunken women.

"'Wallace, look what you've come to!' my sister pleaded. 'Why don't you be a man and pull yourself out of this? You can only sink lower than you are.'

"'Oh, it's no use,' he shrugged a reply, 'I'm done; the booze has got me; I just *can't* stop.'

"'But have you ever tried God, Wallace? Have you ever given Him a chance to help you?'

"The man shook his head. 'No,' he admitted slowly, 'I've not tried that.'

"My sister then asked Wallace to get down on his knees. Just then a woman came downstairs with an empty pail in which to get beer from the corner saloon; she stopped, astounded at the sight of Wallace on his knees. But he did not stir, and she staggered out, surprised beyond speech, while my sister and Wallace prayed to God for deliverance.

"The following Sunday he came to her Bible class, but without the Bible she had given him.

"'We all have our own Bibles, Wallace,' she reminded him. 'I would like you to go home and get yours.'

"He went and got his Bible. His old friends were lined up along the street, and as he passed with the Bible under his arm, they jeered and hooted and laughed. 'Aw, he won't stick,' they said, 'he's one o' us.'

"But he did stick!

"Today," Doctor Kelly resumed after a pause, "Wallace is a highly respected man. He owns his own happy home and has a fine son and daughter. He is an effective public speaker, a leader in his section—in short, a substantial, upright, Christian citizen. And that is but half the story.

"Wallace, now a redeemed man, went after his old brother-chum, MacLellan. But MacLellan only sneered, too weak to make that break which Wallace had made in the face of the jeers of the neighborhood. Wallace pleaded with him to face about and took him into his own home. He introduced MacLellan to new friends and for months at a time supported him outright at a heavy personal sacrifice. Wallace was determined to win him.

"But MacLellan remained deaf to him, and instead of heeding he deliberately became worse and worse, and at last unspeakable in his vileness.

"As Wallace's daughter grew into womanhood, realizing his duty to her, he had to ask 'Mac' to leave his house. For more than twenty-five years Wallace had worked to save his friend and apparently had failed. At last MacLellan dropped completely out of sight.

"Then one late fall day, now about a year ago, word reached Wallace that 'Mac' was in the Philadelphia Almshouse. He went to him at once and found him segregated in a ward, the final resting place of the dregs and derelicts of the city, a broken, penniless, embittered old man, fast becoming blind. MacLellan cursed and reviled him while he cursed the world and society which he blamed for his lot; he hated the sight of Wallace in his prosperity.

"But Wallace went back again and again, until at last something extraordinary happened inside MacLellan. It was a day or so before New Year when Wallace came to my sister.

"'Mrs. Bradford,' he said, 'I'm going to bring my old friend 'Mac' to your Watch Night services at the Lighthouse on New Year's Eve.'

"'I shall be glad to see him,' she replied. And from one of the tables at the Lighthouse meeting rooms, New Year's Eve, a man called her by name. She turned to see a stranger, the face of a man who seemed supremely happy. She tried hard to place that face, sure that she knew every man present, until at last, recalling Wallace and his promise to bring 'Mac,' she realized this man must be MacLellan.

"Even the old lines, she told me afterward, had left MacLellan's countenance; the leering, evil, embittered look had gone—in its place there had come a certain sweetness and, above all, a radiating joy. Before her was a man built anew, changed so completely that no resemblance to the man she had known remained. And when she mentioned his approaching blindness he said, 'Thank God! I had to become blind in order to see.'

"MacLellan will probably regain some measure of sight," Doctor Kelly added. "But whatever the outcome of the operation, another light than that of day has come to him, and he can declare with the man in the Bible, in the highest of all senses, 'Whereas I was blind, I now see.'"

13

DR. ROBERT LAWS:
Missionary Extraordinary

A lexander Gammie, writing in 1934, said, "Dr. Robert Laws was frequently referred to as the greatest living missionary, and now that he is dead his name is assured of an enduring place on the roll of fame. He will rank with those great missionary pioneers, John G. Paton of the New Hebrides, James Chalmers of New Guinea, and even with David Livingstone, whose mantle fell upon his shoulders. . . . His services were recognized by the King, acknowledged by Government, and applauded by the nation. It is, said one who knew him well, the truth that he was unique among missionary pioneers, administrators, and statesmen. In variety of attainments, in capacity for all forms of work, in indomitable faith and patience, and in magnificent practical achievement no one has surpassed him. He possessed as much courage as David Livingstone and certainly as much faith and endurance" (*Famous Preachers I Have Heard*).

J. H. Morrison, who saw firsthand his work in Africa, reported how Laws, after years of struggle, established a center at Chitambo, the remote spot where Livingstone died. He speaks of the spiritual harvest "which commanded the attention of the whole Christian world and made Livingstonia famous as one of the most wonderful triumphs of modern missions. . . . Laws has seen and done more wonderful things than, perhaps, any other living man."

Then Morrison refers to the famous Henry Drummond, who also experienced an extended stay with Laws in Africa, who, in introducing Laws to a great crowd of students in Edinburgh, said, "No man in Europe was better worth listening to." Drummond further spoke of "the glory of the work" carried on "in a beastly climate." Then we read, "The speaker rose, a rugged, burly form, in striking contrast to the elegant figure and delicate complexion of the Professor. 'One had no time to think of the glory of the work,' he [Laws] said; 'it was just a case of pegging away in one's shirt sleeves from day to day. As for the climate, well, look at him and, look at me, and judge for yourselves'!" (*The Missionary Heroes of Africa*).

The *Wycliffe Biographical Dictionary of the Church* mentions Laws (1851–1934) as laboring "in Africa for fifty-two years," a remarkable record for unhealthy pioneer days. Further, he was "elected Fellow of the Royal Geographical Society" and earlier was made "Moderator of the General Assembly of the United Free Church of Scotland," an unprecedented distinction for a missionary.

Although from Scotland, Laws was not a stranger to our continent. Traveling widely here for new ideas to carry to Africa, on his third American trip he spoke at one of the famous Northfield conferences and left a strong impression.

Allow this further pointed citation. Robert Hall Glover, in *The Progress of World-Wide Missions*, says, "The Livingstonia Mission is the most distinguished of all memorials to Livingstone. It now occupies the whole western shore of Lake Nyasa. Dr. Robert Laws, the leader of its pioneer party and still in active service [1924], has all along been the outstanding figure of this remarkable work. The trials and vicissitudes heroically met and overcome, and the ultimate progress and spiritual victories achieved, are ones which have seldom been equaled in missionary literature."

My brother, while pursuing graduate studies at the University of Edinburgh, Scotland, met Dr. Laws, and Laws presented him a copy of the book, *Laws of Livingstonia*, which he personally autographed for him, dating his signature, May 20, 1929. The book of nearly four hundred tightly packed pages by W. P. Livingstone was written some years earlier and does not complete the good man's service in

Africa, but from it can be drawn much of the story of this man's remarkable life and labors.

Robert Laws was born into a humble but pious home in Scotland, dedicated from birth to be a missionary. His mother, however, died when he was but two years old, and he was brought up by "a somewhat strict" stepmother. In early youth he was apprenticed as a cabinet maker. Reading Livingstone's *Travels*, he was fired with an ambition to be a missionary. From a poor family, it was a real struggle, but by dint of frugal living and hard manual labor at long hours by day followed by evening classes, he achieved entrance to the University of Aberdeen, where in seven years he actually completed degrees in Arts, in Medicine, and in Theology.

Inquiring into the needs of central Africa, he determined that a boat on the extensive Lake Nyasa would be the most feasible approach (no adequate roads or maps then existed). To get a suitable boat to the lake, it would have to be designed in pieces, carried over hills and river rapids, then assembled and riveted together with its wood burning boiler and engine. Laws therefore studied mechanics and kindred subjects. Years later, even after turning the boat over to others, he was occasionally called away from pressing duties to repair and restart the engine. And on the field he constructed with his own hands (with minimal assistance from natives) schools, printing plants, water-works, grain mills, a saw mill, a hospital and dispensary, etc. On top of all this he edited and published a missionary magazine, learned several native languages, served as interpreter for government officials, and translated and saw through the press a sizable amount of Scripture in tribal languages, one tongue requiring five years for the gospel of Mark.

Laws' early years in Africa were marked by loneliness, recurring debilitating sickness, attacks by wild animals, threats on his life by slave traders and warring chiefs, frustrations over long delayed supplies and breakdowns of equipment, defection of laboriously trained native workers, restrictions imposed by empire builders, territorial claims by other societies, death after death of consecrated missionaries sent out to assist, leaving the doctor all alone (he built many a coffin with his own hands and dug many a grave himself). At times when he was laid low by fever and dysentery, he would be called to minister to the dying—white and black alike—and would arise and struggle, though rain-soaked, to the place of need, ministering to the dying and comforting the bereaved, all the time holding up Christ before everyone.

The foundation for all this was laid in his childhood and youth. In the biography referred to, we read that his own mother "was consumptive, and when only twenty-four she sickened, and one Sunday evening lay dying. . . . As she lay in her coffin, his father took the child and raised him up that he might gaze upon her. The sight of the white, still face haunted his memory ever after.

"He found a second home with his grandparents. Here he obtained his first lessons in reading, the textbooks being the Shorter Catechism and the metrical Psalms. One picture comes clear-cut out of the haze of those days—of his grandmother standing over the fire and stirring with one hand the strawberry jam which simmered in the pot slung from the iron swivel and with the other urging him on with the task of learning the 84th Psalm, while all the time his thoughts and eyes were occupied longingly with the sweet-smelling preserve."

Later, with his father again we read, "In this difficult period the chief influences molding his character were those operating in his own home. His father was an exceptional man, a childlike disciple of the Master he loved. 'One of the saintliest men I have ever known,' a distinguished member of the congregation has said.

"His stepmother was different. She was the product of a spiritual temperature rendered frigid by Calvinism. Life to her was very serious and governed by stern principles to which allegiance must be given at all costs. Her creed, reacting on her character, made her seem cold, severe, unsympathetic. In reality, she had a heart of gold; love burned within her, but it was damped down and seldom glowed on the surface. She did not understand her stepson. Determined to do her duty faithfully by him, she sought to drive rather than to lead him into the ways of righteousness. He did not fathom her motives and dumbly resented her methods. He missed something; he could not tell what.

"Mr. Laws [the father] entered service in cabinet making, and life for the family became more of a strain and struggle than it had been. The boy was observant and thoughtful, and he came to the conclusion that it was his duty to leave school and assist his parents. He had resolved to be a missionary, but he saw no present prospect of accomplishing his purpose and made no mention of the matter to his father. The bitterness of the decision for Robert soon passed, and he did not give up hope. Deep in his heart he determined that he would yet win through.

"He continued his tasks in the shop where his conscientiousness would not allow him to scamp any duty or do any but honest and efficient work. The place was as much his study as his home. He drew the problems of Euclid on the walls and worked them out while busy with his tools.

"Another kind of problem came into his head one day. Was he saved or not? Puzzled, he stood thoughtfully at the bench and considered the matter. His eye caught a diagram on the wall; it was an inspiration to his practical mind. 'I will reason it out,' he said, with the ghost of a smile at his own whimsicality. 'This is the proposition—Believe in the Lord Jesus Christ and thou shalt be saved. All those, therefore, who believe are saved; I must either believe or not believe. Do I believe? Yes I do. Therefore I am saved.' From that time he never had a doubt as to his position."

Dr. Laws' recognition of the saving work of Christ being basic stood through years of toil in Africa. More than three hundred pages through the biographical record, we read, "The foundations—roads, water, light, and power—were now laid. To him they were but the stepping-stones to higher things—means to an end; the real purpose of all his endeavor, the evangelizing of Livingstonia. He never slackened in his anxious solicitude for the moral and spiritual welfare of those under his care. 'All the work of our little community,' he wrote, 'converges toward its great central purpose of winning natives to Christ.'"

We conclude with this moving incident. "One day a man was carried in. The doctor was lying ill, but he rose and found that the leg had been smashed. There was nothing to do but to amputate. 'No, no,' said the patient, 'I don't want my leg taken away.' 'Then you will die,' replied the Doctor; 'you are half dead already.' But neither he nor his friends would consent to the operation. As the man lay bleeding to death he cried repeatedly, 'I am going, white man! Where am I going, white man?'

"'Ay, whither away!' echoed the Doctor sadly, and for days could not get the words out of his mind."

14

JERRY MCAULEY:
River Thief Turned
Rescue Mission Pioneer

City "rescue missions" got their beginning with a man named Jerry McAuley. He was a thief and a robber, a drunkard, blasphemer, convict in prison, and afterward an outcast and an outlaw. The desperate and reckless life he led as bounty-broker, gambler, prize-fighter, rough, drunkard, and river thief left an unmistakable impress upon him. He was hard and hopeless. But this once despised and hunted river thief was transformed by the blessed Savior into a man whose principal aim was the salvation of outcast men and women; for this he labored and thought and prayed, but his work had a reflex influence which spread out through all classes, and by means of it hundreds of refined and cultivated people were led to Christ.

His autobiography referred to was titled, *Transformed: The History of a River Thief.* In it we read, "I was born in Ireland. Our family was broken up by sin, for my father was a counterfeiter and left home to escape the law before I knew him. I was placed at a very early age in the family of my grandmother. My first recollections of her are of her counting her beads and kissing the floor for penance. I would take the opportunity while she was prostrated upon her face, to throw things at her head in mischievous play, and when she rose from her knees, it was to curse and swear at me. . . . I was never taught or sent to school but left to have my own way, to roam about in idleness, doing mischief continually.

"At the age of thirteen I was sent to this country, to the care of a married sister in New York City. . . . After a while I felt I could live by my own wits and left my sister's home to take care of myself. I earned what I could and stole the rest to supply my daily wants.

"We had a boat, by means of which we boarded vessels in the night, stealing whatever we could lay our hands on. Here I began my career as a river thief. In the daytime we went up into the city and sold our ill-gotten goods and then spent our time as long as our money lasted in the vile dens of Water Street, practicing all sorts of wickedness. Here I learned to be a prize-fighter and by degrees rose through all the grades of vice and crime, till I became a terror and nuisance in the fourth ward.

"I was only nineteen years of age when I was arrested for highway robbery—a child in years, but a man in sin. . . . I was sentenced to fifteen years. I burned with vengeance. I was handcuffed and sent in the cars to Sing-Sing. When I arrived at the prison—I shall never forget it—the first thing that attracted my attention was the sentence over the door: 'The way of the transgressors is hard.' . . . But God was more merciful to me than man. His pure eyes had seen all my sin, and yet He pitied and loved me and stretched out His hand to save me. . . .

"I had been in prison four or five years when, one Sunday morning, I went with the rest to a service in the chapel. I was moody and miserable. As I took my seat, I raised my eyes carelessly to the platform, and who should I see there beside the chaplain but a man named Orville Gardner, who had been for years a confederate in sin. 'Awful Gardner' was the name by which I had always known him. Since my imprisonment, he had been converted and was filled with desire to come to the prison, that he might tell the good story to the prisoners. I could not have been more surprised.

"He came down and stood on the floor that he might be among the men. He told them it was only a little while since he had taken off the stripes which they were then wearing. . . . I do not believe there was a dry eye in the whole crowd. Tears filled my eyes. I knew this man was no hypocrite. We had been associated in many a dark deed and sinful pleasure. I had heard oaths and curses, vile words from his mouth, and I knew he could not talk as he did then unless some great, wonderful change had come to him. I devoured every word. One sentence impressed me deeply which he said was a verse from the Bible. The Bible! I knew there was such a book. I had never read a word in it. But now God's time had come, and He was going to show me treasures that were hidden in that precious book.

"I went back to my cell. How dreary is Sunday in prison; the rest of the day is spent in solitude. What I had heard was ringing in my ears, and the thought possessed me to find the verse which had so struck me. Every prison cell is supplied with a Bible, but alas, few of them are used. Mine I had never touched since the day I entered my narrow apartment, and I had laid it away in the ventilator. I took it down, beat the dust from it, and opened it. But where to find the words I wanted I knew not. There was nothing to do but to begin and read till I came to them. On and on I read. How interested I grew. I became fascinated, and night after night I read by the dim light which came from the corridor. I never found that verse. I had forgotten it in my new interest in the book. But I found a good many verses that made me stop and think. . . .

"I was resting one night from reading, walking up and down and thinking what a change religion had made in Gardner, when I began to have a burning desire to have the same. I could not get rid of it, but what could I do? Something within me said, 'Pray.' I couldn't frame a prayer. The voice within said, 'Go to God; He will tell you what is right.'

"What a struggle I went through! I knew I ought to pray, but I felt myself blushing. Every sin stared me in the face. I recollected the 'Whosoever' in the Bible. 'That means you,' said the inward voice. 'But I'm so wicked,' I urged. To every thought that came up there came a verse of Scripture. I fell on my knees and was so ashamed I jumped up again. This conflict went on for three or four weeks. It was fearful. I wonder now at the long-suffering of God. But at last the Lord sent a softness and tenderness into my soul. I shed many tears. I cried unto the Lord.

"I fell on my knees on the hard stone floor of my cell, resolved to stay there, whatever might happen, till I found forgiveness. I was desperate. Sweat rolled off my face in great drops. Oh, how I longed for God's mercy! Just then in the height of my distress, it seemed as if a hand was laid upon my head, and these words came to me, 'My son, thy sins which are many are forgiven.' Oh, the precious Christ! How plainly I saw Him lifted up for my sins. What a thrill went through me. I jumped from my knees; I paced up and down in my cell. A heavenly light seemed to fill it. I clapped my hands and shouted, 'Praise God! Praise God!'

"One of the guards was passing along the corridor and called out, 'What's the matter?' 'I've found Christ,' I answered; 'my sins are all forgiven. Glory to God!' He took out a piece of paper from his pocket and wrote the number of my cell and threatened to report me in the morning. But I didn't care for that. My soul was all taken up with my great joy. But the next morning nothing happened to me, and I think the Lord made him forget it.

"What a night that was! I shall surely never forget the time when the Lord appeared as my gracious Deliverer from sin. From that time life was all new to me. I was happy, for Jesus was my friend; my sins were washed away, and my heart was full of love and thanksgiving. I hated every sinful way. I had smoked, but something within me now said it was wrong, and I gave it up. . . ."

Yes, the change was evident to those around him; his witness bore fruit in the conversion of other prisoners. Finally, the governor gave him a full pardon, restoring him to citizenship.

With most everything against parolees in those days, Jerry had a dreadful struggle after being released; he fell back into his old ways a couple of times, but God finally gave him permanent victory, acknowledged by all. He began a rescue mission for such as he had been, which became famous for years as the "Jerry McAuley Mission." And before he died at age forty-five, he undertook the establishment of still another such mission.

Many years later these missions were the inspiration for William Borden ("Borden of Yale") in establishing a mission in New Haven, Connecticut. As Borden's biography states, "What could the unbeliever make of a man who had been the terror of the worst ward in New York, a river thief who would not have hesitated, as he himself said, 'to cut a man's throat for a five dollar bill and kick him overboard,' who was sentenced to fifteen years hard labor in Sing-Sing when he was only nineteen, with no power to break his chains—until Christ met and transformed him? Yet that man was

Jerry McAuley, who established in his old haunts the first of such Rescue Missions."

And attorney I. H. Linton bears this witness, "It is well known that 'long continued use of alcohol or morphine produces an abnormal condition of the stomach, nerves, and tissues which makes an instantaneous cessation of a drug craving physiologically impossible,' as the doctor protested to Jerry McAuley when he testified about his conversion. The doctor's protest elicited the famous reply from McAuley, 'Praise the Lord! I knew He had given me a new heart, but I didn't know He had given me a new stomach too.' When Jerry was asked how he knew he was converted, his answer was, 'Bless you, I was there when it happened.'"

15

DR. JOSEPH MCCABA:
Missionary Teacher

McCaba's biography, *The Teacher Who Laughs*, takes its title from the nickname given him by the African natives among whom he labored so long and effectively (Regular Baptist Press, Schaumburg, Illinois). From the back cover of the book we read, "Dr. Joseph McCaba was born and reared in Paterson, New Jersey. From the day of his conversion he was an active witness for his Lord.

"Answering the call of God to become a missionary, he labored in the Republic of Niger (French Sudan). He studied the languages and was able to converse in Arabic, French, and several African dialects. He reduced the Dierma language to writing and translated the New Testament to give them the Word of God.

"Dr. McCaba was an outstanding diplomat. He was greatly esteemed by officials of the French government and diplomatic representatives of Niger, Mali, and Algeria. He was decorated by the president of Niger.

"Dr. McCaba was the founder of Evangelical Baptist Missions (headquartered in Kokomo, Indiana)."

We take the story of McCaba's conversion from his own words as found in this biography.

"'Let's see what those nuts are doing,' Tom exclaimed one day. He referred to four men who met regularly at noon in a small room adjacent to the dyehouse where they were employed in Paterson, New Jersey.

"Tom and I had joined the Navy together toward the end of the First World War. Following our discharge from service, we continued to be buddies. We each had found work at the same company and generally ate lunch together. On that particular day we each washed our lunch down with a quart of wine supplied by some of the workers in that silk-finishing and dyeing establishment.

"Tom worked in the folding department as foreman; I was time-keeper and paymaster. We both felt the authority of our positions and thought that somehow we would get back at these men for their constant preaching. They were thorns in our sides, especially when they told us we weren't 'saved' and we had to accept Christ into our hearts. How could a person accept Christ into his heart? It sounded crazy.

"Anyway, the dyehouse was no place to preach religion. That is why churches were built. Besides, we considered ourselves as religious as those men were.

"We found the men sitting on piles of raw silk. Tom and I seated ourselves in one of the three-cubic-foot pigeonholes which lined the walls. The men knew we were not there for any good. But they welcomed us cordially and began their meeting.

"Little did they realize to what extent our opposition would go. When they began to sing a hymn, we sang the same tune with parodies out of our filthy hearts. When they read the Bible, we interrupted with quotations from the prayer book or with some philosophy we had learned.

"Finally, as they began to pray, we mocked them, cursed and swore at them. And we were only three feet away.

"This continued for six months every day of the six day workweek. Often, one of them would see me in the shop and seek to testify, arousing my inordinate temper. I exploded with oaths, which today I wish never had been uttered. . . .

"One day Tom was sick, and I decided to have some fun by myself. I sat in the same pigeonhole I had used for six months, but curiously, I felt something strange was about to take place.

"The men sang their hymn, read the Bible, and prayed without any interruption. Being alone, my courage was gone. I could not ridicule; I could not spew out foul language as I had done so often. A power seemed to grip me which kept my mouth shut.

"One of the men, the Irishman, asked me if he could sing a hymn for me. He had a beautiful tenor voice. I told him to go ahead if it would make him happy. With tears streaming down his face, he sang:

> How tender and sweet was the Master's voice
> As He lovingly called to me:
> 'Come over the line, it is only a step,
> I am waiting, my child, for thee.'
>
> 'Over the line,' hear the sweet refrain.
> Angels are chanting the heavenly strain.
> 'Over the line,' why should I remain,
> With a step between me and Jesus?

"As he finished the chorus, I felt that someone had thrust his hand down my throat and was tugging at my heart. I came 'over the line.' In that split second, something changed. Everything seemed different.

"When I returned to my office, the secretary asked what had happened. I told her I was saved, and she said, 'You, too?' From that time on I never told her another filthy story which had become a daily habit.

"When Tom found out, he classified me as 'a nut' along with the others, though with not so much emphasis.

"On the Saturday prior to my conversion I had made a date with a girl friend to take her to a notorious dancehall. The community's worst characters gathered there, and each dance would break up in a fight.

"This was my first experience of the conflict between the old nature and the new nature. There was an inner voice that kept insisting that the dancehall was not a place where a Christian should be found. Another force insisted that I should be a gentleman and keep my promise. I decided to meet the girl.

"We had just started dancing when I told her what had happened to me the previous day. She threw it off by saying that I had become religious. I sought to convince her that Jesus Christ now controlled me and that I belonged to Him.

"She retorted, 'What are you doing here?'

"I offered to see her home, but she assured me she knew the way. I left her in the middle of the floor and walked out, cutting off more of the world which had bound me."

So the change was genuine and permanent. Brother McCaba henceforth joined groups in witnessing, went on preaching missions, and finally answered the call to the foreign mission field. And on, amid trials and hardships requiring great courage, to become the missionary statesman where he left his mark.

Taken from *The Teacher Who Laughs* by Joseph McCaba. Copyright © 1973, Regular Baptist Press. Used by permission.

16

BAXTER MCLENDON:
A Marlboro Man's Transformation

Upon being told of the early wild, desperate life of Baxter McLendon, it appears appropriate to emphasize his completely changed nature. Although he is pictured as a preacher with a shaggy head of hair, a heavy drooping mustache, and what seems to be a stern, grim face, yet no less a person than the well-known "Bud" Robinson says of him, "He is as cultured and refined as a university professor. His language is chaste and classic. He does not deal in vulgarities and never utters a word that would give offense to the most delicate. He is a velvety-natured gentleman." But it was not always so.

McLendon's previously dubious ways seemed so deeply embedded in his character that the wonder of it is that there ever was a change. After the change came and his call to preach, he presented the gospel with such fervor that they called him "Cyclone Mack." Indeed, "Bud" Robinson says of him, "He is a unique personage, dramatic in manner, unconventional in style, fearless in his denunciation of sin. . . ." What a transformation! For in his old days the sheriff where he lived said, "He is the most dangerous man in Marlboro County."

McLendon tells his own story in a lengthy message in a volume of his sermons. Only highlights can here be presented.

As a mere lad McLendon felt that he was called to preach. But he stubbornly resisted it. He tells the story. "I made up my mind that I would leave home where heads were bowed at the table and grace said, and where we were all sent to bed from an altar of prayer and an open Bible. When I left home I had just one purpose in view, to get out of Christian environments and holy surroundings and kill my conscience. . . . It made no difference if it was in a gambling hall, barroom, courthouse—everywhere and every place I would go God was there.

"At one time in South Carolina I had been tried in the state court on two or three counts for selling liquor illegally. They had convicted me and I paid the fine. Now they had me in the United States Court and a friend went on my bond. A merchant in our town upbraided him for doing so and told him that he was protecting lawbreakers and encouraging lawlessness. When I heard it I went over and told Capt. Rogers, who had been our sheriff for twenty years and was now ex-sheriff, that I was going to kill this man. He begged me not to do it and told me it was much easier to get into trouble than it was to get out. I said, 'Captain, if the gallows was already built here on the public square and my coffin under it, I'd kill this man.' He said, 'All right, Mack, if you feel that way about it, but make a dead shot because he is a brave man, and if you don't he will get you.'

"I walked across the public square to a revenue officer who had been protecting me, and I said, 'I want you to exchange guns with me. I have some fancy work to do and yours is larger caliber than mine and will do better service.' He tried to persuade me not to do it.

"Think of what a cold-blooded, vicious, demonized, devilized, human being that sin had degenerated me into. I walked down the street about thirty yards, turned to the right a few steps, pulled out my gun and shot this man. I can see the red spot right now over his heart the minute the pistol fired. I saw him stagger. I was confident that I had killed him.

"I ran through the store, crossed the lot, and jumped in a buggy and ran the horse five miles down the road, jumped out and went into one of those dark, dismal, South Carolina swamps. I stayed there until two o'clock that night. I could hear the buggies crossing the bridges and the feet of the horses as they ran up and down the roads. I knew that a great crowd was looking for me. Late that night I crawled out of the swamp and to a friend's house. I rapped on the door, and when he saw me he staggered back and said, 'My God,

Baxter, what did you do that for? You've killed one man and mortally wounded another.'

"I said, 'Well, I didn't intend to kill but one.'

"He said, 'Mack, there are a thousand people looking for you. Just a few moments ago the sheriff and three men came through the yard. Get in that swamp and stay there until night again. I'll go to town and find out all the particulars, and you meet me at that shed about ten or eleven o'clock tonight.'

"I went into the swamp, 'way back out there on a little island among canebrakes and bamboos. If ever God talked to a man, He talked to me that day. Oh, how that monitor in my breast, that telephone from the skies, lashed and lacerated me that day!

"Late that night I crawled out of the swamp and up a corn row to this shed where I promised to meet my friend. Just as I arrived he walked up and said, 'Mack, I have good news for you—you only shot one man, and the doctor says there is a chance for him to live.' I said to him, 'I'm going to Bennettsville and give up.' He said, 'No, Mack, don't you do it. Excitement is high, public opinion is against you, and if they catch you it will mean twenty years at least in the penitentiary.' . . .

"I beat my way to Jefferson County, Ohio, and went to work in the Long Run coal mines on the night shift. . . . I went to southern Florida and opened up one of the lowest-down groggeries or beer joints and gambling hells that the imagination of man can conceive. . . . Everywhere and every place that I would go I was haunted with the thought that my life was a failure. . . ."

After some years he was found back in Bennettsville, his shady friends having worked in his behalf, now proprietor of a barber shop which served as a front for gambling and other questionable operations. He says, "I had gone down the sin line until my brain was clouded by dissipation, a moral derelict, home a hell, mother's heart broken, father's hopes blighted."

He relates, "Brown, who managed my shop, passed by my father's home and my mother called him and asked him how I was getting along. Brown told her that I was going at the same old gait, and he said she looked at him and the tears ran down her face and she sobbed and said, 'Baxter, I believe, is gone. We have held on to God for him for years, and it seems now that he has passed redemption.' She said a revival was going to begin in Bennettsville in a few days."

"Brown came to the shop and told me the conversation he had with my mother, how she wept over my lost condition. I told him I had troubles of my own and never to mention to me anything that people said about me. But when I thought of my old broken-hearted mother with her tear-stained face, weeping over my dissipated life, I'll tell you it hung like a black cloud in the sky of my happiness.

"The day arrived when they began to erect the old tent about 75 yards from my place of business. I can see it going up now. That night they had their first service. I wasn't interested. I closed my shop at 8 o'clock, and, none of the local talent being on hand for a game, I went over to the hotel to see if there were any traveling men that I could corral and bring in, but they were conspicuous by their absence. I waited a while, but they didn't show up. I said, 'Well, that meeting is the biggest thing in town, and I'll go over and round them up.' I went over to the tent and took a seat 'way back in the rear. I don't think I heard a word the preacher said; I was so busy taking inventory of the congregation to see if there was enough of my kind to have a game after the service.

"After the sermon they made the altar call, and Bud Robinson stepped off the rostrum and pushed his way through the great crowd and walked over benches until he reached me. He stood there and gazed at me, and I stared at him. I have often wished I could reproduce his tender tone and loving look when he said, 'Young man, a man that looks like you and has the appearance that you have—the devil is doing dirt with him in this country.' He turned and walked back to the rostrum without saying a word to another soul. Some girls standing near me said, 'Baxter, did he know you?' 'No, he never saw me before.' 'Well that is strange.'

"I forgot about my anticipated poker game, and I opened up in high gear for home. I retired for the night, but not to sleep. The pillow was hard, the bed uncomfortable, the cover too short. I rolled and tumbled. . . ." All he could think about was the words Robinson had spoken to him. "How my conscience talked to me that long, lonely night. Rena, my wife, said, 'Baxter, what have you done? Your conscience is lashing you, and you have rolled and turned and groaned all night long.'

"Next morning I got up and went down to my place of business. I took a drink. Brown, my manager, came in and he said, 'Why Mack, what is the matter with you? I have never seen a man in the state of mind you are in. You are cursing these boys and everything in the community.' I would go back in the rear, take a drink, go out and walk the streets, and I would catch myself wringing my hands and groaning. I damned preachers; I cursed churches, trying to make myself believe that I wasn't interested and under conviction."

In those days they also had morning revival meetings. McLendon continues, "At eleven o'clock I said, 'Boys, I believe I will go over yonder and see what those ginks have to say.' I used that slang to throw them off and make them think I wasn't interested." But the preaching got under his skin, and he attended several more meetings, even going down and kneeling at the altar for a bit.

After a meeting, he says, "I walked down to the shop, and as I entered every fellow went on dress parade. They stared and gazed and looked like I was a whole menagerie. I got me a paper, leaned up against the wall, and put it up before my face. I didn't know whether it was right side up or not. All afternoon people were coming in from up town to the shop and walking in and the fellows would say, 'Have a seat.' They would say, 'No, we are just walking around.'"

As more meetings were attended, things that were wrong in his life came up, and he had a fearful struggle to be willing to give up one after another. Not, of course, that that alone would save him. But each meeting brought deeper conviction and created a greater sensation in the town.

Finally, "I had come to the last service of the meeting; the last sermon had been preached, the last song had been sung. I was there at the altar. Father and mother were on one side of me, Rena on the other, the preachers standing around me. They had said everything that they knew to say to me. I started out with Rena by my side. Father and Mother were looking on with disappointed and broken hearts.

"Just then I met a little woman and she said, 'Baxter, have you surrendered?' I said, 'No.' She said, 'You poor, hard-hearted, cold-blooded, vicious fellow! This meeting is a bell of destiny tolling out your death knell. It may be your last call.' I clinched my hands, I bit my lips, I gazed out into illimitable space, and I said, 'Oh God, here goes.'

"I knew I was saved. I turned to Rena and I said, 'The work has been done!' Ma said, 'What did he say?' Rena said, 'He is saved!' Ma was not of the emotional kind; she was of the old Reformed Presbyterian stock. But Ma shouted her hat off and her hair down. I'll never forget the shine that was on that old face and the sparkle that was in her eye. The Christians grabbed me up in their arms. When they put me down, I jumped up on a high bench and said, 'Farewell, boys, I am done.'

"I walked into my little home, and to show you what a cold-blooded, hard-hearted, heartless devil I had been, I walked over to the cradle and picked up my baby that was eighteen months old that I had never had in my arms before. I pressed him against my bosom, kissed his face, dropped a tear on his cheek. . . .

"The next morning I walked down the street, and the first man I met was the high sheriff. He grabbed me by the hand and said, 'Mack, I congratulate you.' This gentleman and I had had a lot of unpleasant business, and up to that time I hadn't felt kindly toward him. Then I went over to see the prosecuting attorney. He could stand before a jury and say, "Mr. Foreman and gentlemen of the jury, there is the most disreputable character that the good county of Marlboro has ever produced. . . .' When I walked into his office that morning he said, 'Mack, it is done; I can see it written all over you.' I said, 'Well, I am under bond for gambling. If you had found me guilty, what would it have cost me?' He said, 'Mack, go on and don't mention it any more. I know that you are converted and gambling will cease because you are the tap root of the whole deviltry.' . . .

"Now what was it that happened to me? I had a resurrected will; a regeneration had arisen in my soul; I was transformed by the power of God."

17

ROBERT MOFFAT:
Livingstone's Trailblazer in Africa

When David Livingstone was buried amid England's greatest kings, statesmen, poets, and sages in Westminster Abbey, the nobles and dignitaries of the day vied with one another for prominent places in the cortege of the state funeral. As the casket bearing the remains of the famous African explorer and missionary was borne slowly down the crowded abbey, a little old man with flowing white beard walked with silent step at the head of the bier. If anyone had asked, "Who is that drab, bent figure leading the solemn procession," the answer might well have been, "Why that is the venerable Robert Moffat, whose own daughter married Livingstone, the man who plunged into Africa's dark lands many years before Livingstone, who explored and pioneered new areas, a truly distinguished missionary in his own right." Indeed, it was he, when on furlough, who young Livingstone heard tell of "the smoke of a thousand villages" without a ray of true light and led the latter to Africa.

That Moffat, after more than fifty years in the dark continent, outlived his famous son-in-law is itself noteworthy. He has been termed "the patriarch of South African missions, a man who had a significant influence in that section of the world for more than half a century" (R. A. Tucker, *From Jerusalem to Irian Jaya*). Another reports of Moffat, "Twice he was presented to Queen Victoria at her request; twice he breakfasted with Gladstone; . . . the senate of Edinburgh University conferred upon him the degree of doctor of divinity; the freedom of the city of London became his privilege. . . . Once crossed to Paris at the invitation of the French Missionary Society and there addressed an audience of four thousand Sunday school children"(E. D. Hubbard, *The Moffats*). All that occurred at an advanced age, for during his fifty-three years of missionary service he took only one furlough to his homeland. (We missionaries today are softies.)

Still further it is recorded, "Everywhere he went his presence excited the strongest interest, for he had come to be regarded by universal consent as 'the venerable father of the missionary world.' . . . On one of his journeys to Scotland he visited the home of his boyhood where he had some amusing encounters with his old school fellows. 'Are you aware, sir,' said the village tailor, 'that if you are really the person you represent yourself to be, you must be the father-in-law of Livingstone the African explorer.' 'And so I am,' said Moffat. The old tailor got to his feet. 'Is it possible,' he exclaimed, 'that the father-in-law of Livingstone stands before me and under my humble roof?'" (J. H. Morrison, *Missionary Heroes of Africa*).

But it was not alone being father-in-law to Livingstone that merited such recognition. Perhaps the first thing that gave him a wide reputation was the conversion of the cruel and notorious outlaw Afrikaner. Plunging north from the Cape area, he ventured where no white man dared to go. "'What! You are going after Afrikaner with a Bible instead of a gun? You must be mad.' An old Boer lady burst into tears when she heard of the missionary's determination. 'Don't go north,' she pleaded. 'Afrikaner is wicked. He will use you as a target for shooting practice. He will use your skin to make a drum. There's not a white man who will go near Afrikaner.' She had lost two sons in tribal warfare, about Moffat's own age" (H. F. Frame, *Roll On, Wagon Wheels*).

"Thrust into the center of several cannibalistic tribes . . . [he] set out for the home of the notorious outlaw, Afrikaner. To the surprise and marvel of everyone, he won the dreaded outlaw to Christ" (*Wycliffe Biographical Dictionary of the Church*). Another reports,

"He was warned against Afrikaner, a native chief whose barbarous crimes had made him a terror. . . . When Moffat reappeared in Capetown, bringing with him the converted savage and outlaw, the sensation produced was profound" (R. H. Glover, *The Progress of World-Wide Missions*).

On journeys as that to Afrikaner's territory, Moffat showed fortitude, adaptability, and genius to improvise. On one occasion "he stumbled into" another missionary's house "half-crazed with thirst and hunger, having been three days without food." On another occasion, "unwittingly, the missionary drank water which the little Bushmen had poisoned to trap game. Once, on a cold night, he dug a hole in the sand and buried himself, all but his head. He had the best sleep of the journey that night." Earlier, "His wagon was decrepit from its long journey from Cape Town. By some device or other Robert must mend its broken joints. So he improvised bellows and tools, welded the iron, and the wagon was good. Gun-locks were also repaired at the missionary's forge" (Hubbard).

After many years he was importuned by a distant chief to come to his tribe. "To become a pioneer at the age of sixty-two is no easy feat. But Robert Moffat, by the constant use of his faculties in adventurous tasks, had kept alive within him the intrepid spirit of boyhood. . . . Early and late the veteran missionary was at work" (Hubbard).

Yet Moffat found time for prodigious literary work. He wrote two books on missionary work in Africa. More, he "mastered the Bechwana language and published a spelling-book, catechism, hymnbook, and finally the entire Bible" (J. G. Lawson, *Famous Missionaries*). "He translated the entire Bible and *Pilgrim's Progress* into a language which he himself had reduced to written form" (Hubbard). And he himself set up the printing press in a primitive land. "He was an evangelist, a translator, an educator, a diplomat, and an explorer . . . one of Africa's greatest missionaries of all time" (Tucker).

In all his labors his faithful wife stood by and was of great help. Life was not easy for her who had been raised in affluent circumstances. In Africa "the rain came through the roof, dust storms lashed dust through the chinks, and dogs sometimes broke through the walls and stole the food" (Frame). Mary Moffat "washed clothes by hand in the river. She overcame her aversion to cleaning the floors with cow dung and even recommended it. 'It lays the dust and kills the fleas which would otherwise breed abundantly,'" she said (Tucker). Yet she bore and raised children who followed their father's missionary career.

Robert Moffat's active and eminently useful life would have been nothing if he had not first come into a vital personal relationship with Jesus Christ. We get some glimpses of how it began, as follows (Hubbard): "When Robert Moffat had left his home in Scotland just before his eighteenth birthday to take his new position as gardener at High Leigh, his mother walked with him to the Firth of Forth from which he was to go by ship to England.

"It seemed like a long separation to the mother and her boy, for England and Scotland were very far apart in those days. Excitement and regret blazed in Robert's eyes as he looked toward the shore and then into his mother's serious face. 'Now Robert,' she said, 'I wish to ask one favor of you before we part. I only ask whether you will read a chapter in the Bible every morning and another every evening?' 'Mother,' interrupted the boy rather indignantly, 'you know I read my Bible.' 'I know you do,' she replied, 'but you do not read it regularly or as a duty you owe to God its author. Now I shall return home with a happy heart, inasmuch as you have promised to read the Scriptures daily. Oh Robert, my son,' and her eyes shone with tears, 'read much in the New Testament. Read much in the Gospels, the blessed Gospels. Then you cannot go astray. If you pray, the Lord Himself will teach you.' The passionate enthusiasm which burned in her own life was soon to catch fire in her son's life with an intensity of which she little dreamed.

"In the days that followed, Robert was tempted to abjure that promise to his mother since its fulfillment brought him but little satisfaction at first and sore uneasiness later on. As he went about his work in the garden at High Leigh, one question harassed him continually. 'What think ye of Christ?' Must he answer that question? 'What think ye of Christ?' Would it give him no peace until he dealt with it fairly and squarely? Perhaps he could dodge its attacks if he should give up reading the Bible. At the thought, his mother's face with its dark, pleading eyes came vividly before him, and he knew he could never break his promise to her, whatever commotion it might cause in his mind.

"One night it seemed as if his sins were piled up into a great mountain and were tumbling down upon him. When he awoke, shivering with terror, he fell on his knees in prayer for the first time in many weeks. The specter of his dream pursued him into the daylight and dogged his steps wherever he went, but there was no one to whom he could confide his misery.

"Every evening he betook himself to his garden lodge and there, in solitude undisturbed, read and reread the New Testament even as his mother had bidden him. As he read, meaning gradually crept into the words which had hitherto seemed so blank. 'Can it be possible that I have never understood what I have been reading?' he exclaimed with a full heart. One passage and then another shown out of the fog until he could see his way straight to Jesus Christ and could read the friendly welcome in His face. Then he had all the light he needed to chase fear from his life forever."

The right beginning for a great life.

18

GEORGE MÜLLER:
The Orphanage Founder's Remarkable Conversion

In virtually every religious encyclopedia and in some secular ones, the name of George Müller is found. Though born and educated in Germany, he is best remembered for the orphanages he established in England. He cared for as many as 2,000 children at one time, and more than 10,000 passed through his homes—all provided for without ever asking anyone for a penny or soliciting funds.

Much has been written on the life and experiences of Müller, but perhaps the most outstanding biography is that by Arthur T. Pierson, *George Müller of Bristol*, which tells the detailed story of his conversion and from which we now select only the highlights.

The story of his wicked boyhood is one long tale of evil-doing and of the sorrow which it brings. Sent away to school, temptation opened wide doors before him. Absent from home, he took one step after another in the path of wicked indulgence. At an expensive hotel he ran up bills until, payment being demanded, he had to leave his best clothes as security. At another hotel he tried the same bold scheme again, until having nothing for deposit, he ran off, but this time was caught and sent to jail. This boy of sixteen was already a liar and thief, swindler and drunkard, accomplished only in crime, a companion of convicted felons and himself in a felon's cell.

He was severely chastised by his father, but his heart was still desperately wicked. By his own confession, behind all formal propriety there lay sin and utter alienation from God. His vices induced an illness which kept him in his room for thirteen weeks. There was no spiritual life to act as a force within, and his vows were forgotten almost as soon as made. His resolves and endeavors were powerless to hold him. It is hard to believe that this young man could lie without a blush and with the air of perfect candor. Such was the man who was accepted as a candidate for holy orders and with permission to preach in the Lutheran establishment. This student of divinity knew nothing of God or salvation and was ignorant even of the gospel plan of saving grace. He met defeat, for he had never yet found the one source and secret of strength. His resolves proved frail as a spider's web, unable to restrain him. The true mainspring of all well-regulated lives was still lacking.

With ill-gotten means and forged passport, he traveled through the Alps. George Müller was very adept at vice. To account plausibly to his father for the use of his allowance, a new chain of lies was readily devised. The sin and misery of three years would not have been chronicled but to make clear that his conversion was a supernatural work. Surely such a man, with such surroundings, could undergo no radical change of character and life without the interventions of some mighty power from above!

George Müller continued on through scenes of sin and many perils as well as two serious illnesses. He was as careless as ever; he did not read the Bible or have a copy of it in his possession; he seldom attended worship. This young man had thus grown to manhood without having learned the rudimental truth that sinners and saints differ not in degree but in kind; that if any man be in Christ, he is a new creation.

One Saturday afternoon a friend said to Müller that he was going that evening to a meeting at a believer's house where a few friends met to sing, to pray, and to read the Word of God. Such a program held out nothing fitted to draw a man of the world who sought his daily gratifications at the card table and in the wine cup, the dance and the drama, and whose companionships were found in dissipated young fellows. And yet George Müller felt at once a wish to go to this meeting, though he could not have told why. There was no doubt a conscious void within him that had never been filled. He expressed the desire to go to the meeting which the friend hesitated to encourage lest such a frivolous and reckless devotee of vicious pleasures might feel ill at ease in such an assembly. However, he called for young Müller and took him to the meeting.

That Saturday evening was the turning point in George Müller's history and destiny. He found himself in strange company, amid novel surroundings, and breathing a new atmosphere. His awkwardness made him feel so uncertain of his welcome that he made some apology for being there. But he never forgot brother Wagner's gracious answer, "Come as often as you please; house and heart are open to you."

All present sat down and sang a hymn. Then a brother (who afterward went to Africa under the London Missionary Society) fell on his knees and prayed for God's blessing on the meeting. That kneeling before God in prayer made an impression upon Müller that he never lost.

A chapter was read from the Word of God. A sermon was read. When, after another hymn, the master of the house prayed, George Müller was inwardly saying, "I am much more learned than this illiterate man, but I could not pray as well as he." Strange to say, a new joy was already springing up in his soul, for which he could have given as little explanation as for his unaccountable desire to go to that meeting. But so it was; and on his way home he could not keep from saying to his friend, "All we saw on our journey to Switzerland and all our former pleasures are nothing compared to this evening."

Whether or not on reaching his own room he himself knelt to pray, he could not recall, but he never forgot that a new and strange peace and rest somehow found him as he lay in bed that night. That Saturday evening was to this young student the parting of the ways. He had so tasted that the Lord is gracious, though he could not account for the new relish for divine things, that three times before the Saturday following he sought the house of brother Wagner, there with the help of the brethren to search the Scriptures.

What have we found to be the initial step in George Müller's spiritual history? In a little gathering of believers where for the first time he saw a child of God pray on his knees, he found his first approach to a pardoning God.

A man that had been so profligate and prodigal must at least begin at conversion to live a changed life. Within George Müller a new Power was at work. There was a distaste for wicked joys and former companions; the frequenting of taverns entirely ceased; old habits of untamed speech were arrested and corrected.

George Müller did not become famous merely because of his remarkable transformation from a wicked and dissolute young man into a mature, orderly adult. He gave himself continually to prayer, and the establishment of orphanages was laid on his heart when he had only the equivalent of fifty cents in his pocket. But as he prayed, the means came in, finally consisting of buildings covering thirteen acres in Bristol, England. His later worldwide travels and lectures were the result of his simple trust in God, his walk by faith, and his exemplification of what God can do through a life wholly yielded to Him.

The *Wycliffe Biographical Dictionary of the Church* gives more details, "When Müller was seventy years old, he and his wife started on an evangelistic tour which lasted nearly seventeen years. It took him to Europe, America, Asia, and Australia. They visited forty-two countries, traveled over two hundred thousand miles, and preached to three million hearers. [After] . . . having handled nearly eight million dollars sent in [unsolicited] for the work, George Müller fell asleep in the Lord at the age of ninety-three."

19

I. V. NEPRASH:
Conversion of a Russian Atheist

In Bible School, a Mr. I. V. Neprash was asked to speak to our student body of four hundred-plus. He gave a remarkable testimony, including how God was working among the Russian people. All of us were deeply touched—it was something we would not soon forget.

Somewhat over fifteen years later, being one of the first missionaries to have returned to the Philippines after World War II, I was much surprised when Mr. Neprash contacted me in the city of Manila. He was seeking sanctuary for homeless Russian and Siberian refugees who seemed to find everything against them in their desperate struggle to find a haven in the West. I marveled at Brother Neprash's courageous and unstinting efforts in behalf of those confronted by great odds. Amid severe persecution, Brother Neprash had spent many years evangelizing and teaching in Russia and then among Russian refugees in many countries.

Here is Mr. Neprash's personal story, abridged, first given in *The Sunday School Times* many years ago and then reprinted in a leaflet by the American Tract Society.

Born of pious parents, I. V. Neprash was taught in all the forms and ceremonies of the church. At the age of fifteen he began to feel that he could succeed in whatever he attempted. A great longing to travel was satisfied to his pleasure.

In his school days, serious trouble arose between a classmate and himself, and he had occasion to take advantage of the advice of his mother: *If you are in difficulty, pray.* In his distress, alone in the dark one night, he got on his knees and repeated the Lord's Prayer thirty times. This did not help. Bitterness filled his heart. This was his last prayer for a long time.

In later years, all his classmates were atheists. His professor of religion, a highly educated man, was a drunkard. He did not permit his students to ask questions. Atheistic literature was plentiful. The reading of this, with several sad experiences, made him an atheist at eighteen.

As a young man of twenty-one, Professor Neprash spoke openly against God for the first time. The essence of his belief was: There is no God, no soul, no after life. The real facts of life were summed up in matter, force, and motion.

Year's of desolation and darkness followed, but one desire possessed him. It became a passion. He must find the unknown truth. He searched for it, reading books, books, books; piles of them, hundreds of them. Different materialistic systems were tried. Each of them looked fine in theory, but when put to the test, collapsed utterly. "What is truth? Where can I find it?"

He traveled from place to place, from country to country, but found no one who could help him. Disappointed and hopeless, he returned to Russia by steamer on the Danube. By this time he was cursing God.

He continued to seek but sought in vain. Things were only growing worse. One day, having come to the end of all, he made up his mind to commit suicide. His revolver was prepared. Why not end it all? In that awful moment, memories of childhood flashed before his vision—and Mother! What would Mother do? Could she bear to lose her son, and in this terrible way? Mother's love won.

He did not read the Bible. Why? It was kept in the Greek church. Its cover was kissed, but it was not read. To him, as well as to the intelligensia, it was a book of fables.

What about the believers? There were a few of them about, but all were simple folk, and this cultured young man had no confidence in their judgment.

The seeking soul is never left long in darkness. At last, after two and a half years of searching, Professor Neprash began to perceive God through a scientific book of astronomy by a German astronomer and mathematician. He was confronted by a dilemma. To believe that this marvelous cosmos came into existence of itself was madness. To know in the subconscious mind that there was a Being who made it all and yet in the conscious mind refuse to recognize this fact was hypocrisy. Stubborn rebellion rose in his soul. But at length he faintly admitted to himself—perhaps a superior Being does exist.

He was soon disturbed by a question. If the Creator fixed definite laws for the motions of the heavenly bodies, would He leave human beings without them? "No," said reason. "What and where are these laws?" And now followed a quest more painful than before. He reasoned, "The heavenly bodies follow certain fixed courses and therefore swing with ease through space with never a collision. There must be principles governing my life." In his perplexity he cried out, "How can I learn the plan for my life? What rules govern it?"

At this period the great idealist Tolstoy appealed to him. The heart of his philosophy is: Love thy neighbor as thyself. What an ideal! It seemed beautiful. Gladly and earnestly he set about filling his soul with love. Surely this must be the ultimate good. But it failed, even when it was practiced in all sincerity. It collapsed when put to the test.

Once again our Russian reasoner took courage and determined to find the ultimate good and to learn what ultimate evil is. Though all looked dark, cold, and empty, inside and outside, he went plodding on, even though an endless road seemed to open before him.

"Study," says Professor Neprash, "brought me to the conclusion that there was something radically wrong." His own verdict was, "I am guilty before myself, the world, and my Creator." Days passed.

It occurred to him to think thus: "Suppose I have found the criterion for good and evil. Suppose I have discovered all the rules and will strictly follow them. What about the past? If I could start a perfect life and continue it, I shall only do what is right and obligatory. There will be nothing in that to atone for the past. Is there something that can rectify the past?" The Greek church had given Professor

Neprash the idea of obligation, but he came to the idea of substitutionary atonement by a process of reasoning. There was a necessity for atonement. Logic brought him to Calvary.

"To know that my Creator in the person of His Son, Jesus Christ, became my substitute, took my place on the cross, 'for Him who knew no sin was made sin for us, that we might become the righteousness of God in Him'—this knowledge was too wonderful for me! I could only thank and praise Him."

Rejoicing, praising his Creator for his new found Savior, two months later he started out in the work of the Lord and by His grace has continued in His service for many years.

You have followed the struggle of a soul out of the darkness of atheism into the kingdom of light!

20

W. P. NICHOLSON:
The Irish Evangelist

William P. Nicholson, dynamic, hard-hitting preacher, unabashed in his language and manner, was regarded by many as too coarse and indelicate in his denunciations of sin. Nicholson declaimed against smartly dressed, smug crowds of churchgoers, boldly telling them that if they did not repent of their sins, they were all bound for hell along with thieves and drunkards. He could turn to prim choir members, as they sat facing the congregation, and—shaking a large, bony finger at them—declare that unless they admitted they were sinners and needed to be born again, they would all end up in the lake of fire along with harlots and murderers!

God used his ministry with many turning to the Lord. Percy Crawford, who went on to found in the Philadelphia area the Young People's Church of the Air, the Pinebrook ministries, and finally King's College in New Jersey, found Christ as his Savior through Nicholson's ministry as did multiplied more.

And how did the big, burly Irish evangelist come to know the Lord? The same story is told in both *They Found the Secret*, by V. R. Edman (long president of Wheaton College, Wheaton, Illinois) and *W. P. Nicholson, Flame for God*, by S.W. Murray (of Belfast, Ireland).

Nicholson was born in Northern Ireland in a family of seven chil-

113

dren. His father was a sea captain who took young William on his first voyage at sea when the lad was only six. William had little taste for learning, so at fifteen he left home and sailed away as an apprentice seaman.

"He sailed around the world, and there were occasions when he faced shipwreck. For some time he worked in a railroad construction gang in South Africa. He was subject to the temptations common to sailors and workmen engaged in pioneer construction, and he often recounted later how dominated and enslaved he became to the desire for strong drink. 'I was most religious when I was drunk,' he often said. . . .

"The two most potent influences in the lives of the Nicholson family were their mother and the church. William used to describe how their mother brought the family to church, a distance of about two miles, walking there and back to the Sunday services. The minister exercised a strong evangelistic ministry, so direct at times that William used to recall occasions when he had to jump over a seat at the end of a service to escape from the minister's pressing attentions."

After a spell abroad he returned home. One morning, while reading the morning paper and smoking and awaiting the breakfast being prepared by his godly mother, suddenly he came under deep conviction of sin. A voice spoke within him urging him to repent and believe on Christ. In desperation he made his decision. Trembling with fear, he cried, "Lord, I yield. I repent of my sins and now accept Thee as my Savior." Then, he says, "Suddenly and powerfully and consciously, I was saved. Such a peace and freedom from fear, such a sweet and sure assurance filled my soul."

"I turned to my mother and said, 'Mother, I am saved.' She looked at me and nearly collapsed, and said, 'When?' I said, 'Just now.' 'Where?' 'Here where I am sitting.' She cried with joy unspeakable. She couldn't say a word, but just hugged me and cried."

"I have never had any doubt about my salvation," he used to say. "I never doubted my dear mother's word about my natural birth, and do you think it strange of me to take God's Word without a doubt or fear? I became a new creature and began hating sin. . . . I was truly born again and a new creature in Christ Jesus. I had the inward witness and the outward evidence that I was a changed man."

Later Nicholson relates, "The Salvation Army had come to our town. The Corps was composed of two wee girls in uniform. They held open-air meetings and made a noise with their tambourines. Their first soldier was a man called 'Daft Jimmy.' He had hardly enough brains to give him a headache, but he had sense enough to get saved. He carried the flag as they marched the streets.

"I was told by Satan that I would have to go to the open-air meeting and march down the street with two wee girls and a fool. That filled me with dread. I would be laughed at by all my friends. I would lose my reputation. I said, 'Lord, I will be willing to go to Timbuctoo or Hong Kong.' I couldn't get out of it. I became desperate.

"I went down to the shore, and there under a clear sky and shining stars I made a complete and unconditional surrender. What a thrill, what a peace, what a joy! Although an old-fashioned Presbyterian, I began to weep and sing and rejoice like an old-fashioned Methodist. . . .

"So I went to the open-air meeting on a Saturday night. As I walked down the street that Saturday, it seemed as if every friend and relative I ever had were out and about. When I came to the open-air meeting and saw the two wee Salvation Army girls singing and rattling their tambourines and poor Daft Jimmy holding the flag, I nearly turned back. I was dying hard that night. I stepped off the footpath and stood in the ring. Then to my horror one of them said, 'Let us get down on our knees and pray.' What could I do? I couldn't run away; so down I got on my knees.

"The crowd gathered around. I could hear their laughter and jeers. The officer prayed short and to the point. I could have wished the prayer had been as long as the 119th Psalm. I stood up blushing and nervous. Then to my horror she said, 'Brother, take this tambourine and lead the march down the street to the Barracks. I couldn't let a girl beat me, so I took it. That did it. My shackles-fell off, and I was free; my fears all gone. I started down the street, I lost my fear of man; joy and peace and glory filled me."

Soon Nicholson was holding his own evangelistic meetings in Northern Ireland. After several years he was invited to the United States to be with J. Wilbur Chapman and Charles M. Alexander in their work. Then he went with them to Melbourne, Sydney, Brisbane, and Adelaide, Australia.

Later Nicholson was back in Ireland, where we read, "In the early nineteen-twenties, the North of Ireland passed through a period of strife and bloodshed following the establishment of a separate

Parliament for Northern Ireland. The times were such that a sense of apprehension and despair gripped the hearts of many and spread. In the mercy of God, an intervention came from an unexpected source. There began a series of evangelistic campaigns which had a profound effect upon the religious and communal life of the Province. An evangelist with his roots in the North of Ireland came back to his homeland at this time." Nicholson's widespread and effective evangelistic campaigns are credited with stemming a tide that might have brought utter chaos to the land. [*Northern Ireland could use another campaign like that today!*—Ed.]

A few characteristics of the man may be noted. "Nicholson was his own business manager, publicity agent, and song leader. When he made his entrance to a meeting he would immediately take charge, lead the singing, conduct the service, make the announcements, and conduct the appeal, as well as preach—not infrequently for up to an hour. In his missions he was a firm believer in making an open appeal for decision at the end of the service. He conducted after-meetings."

One observer reports, "I have seen his vast audiences convulsed with laughter, cheering uproariously, and within ten seconds sitting in solemn stillness under the spell of his pathos." Another, in one and the same sentence, refers to "his terrific severity" and to "his motherlike tenderness." Contrast was also found in the varieties who thronged his meetings, from "people of leisure and wealth, students in our universities, and employers of labor," to "gangs that lounged at street corners." In East Belfast it was reported that workmen "marched to the church straight from the shipyard. So great was the crush at the entrance to the church building that the pillar supporting the gates was moved off its foundation. . . . A foreman in the shipyard remarked, 'Now you would think you were working in a Sunday school,' so marked was the change in the atmosphere and the absence of swearing."

We close with this statement from Dr. Edman regarding Nicholson, "He has journeyed around the world more than ten times and witnessed for the Savior in nearly every land on the face of the earth. Tens of thousands have come to the Savior in his evangelistic preaching. . . ."

21

ARTHUR TAPPAN PIERSON:
Pastor, Editor, Authority on Missions

Arthur T. Pierson has been characterized as "a pastor, editor, writer, and missionary advocate," and "devoted to evange- listic activity, scriptural preaching." (*Wycliffe Biographical Dictionary of the Church*). Speaking of missionary interests, another writing during his lifetime refers to his being "editor of the *Missionary Review of the World* and is considered the leading authority on missions" (Frederich Barton).

A. T. Pierson's name appears as one of the contributing editors of the long-popular *Scofield Reference Bible*.

Pierson was widely known on both sides of the Atlantic. He was perhaps the first and certainly one of the few Americans asked to actively participate in and speak at the English Keswick conference center.

When C. H. Spurgeon's health began to fail, Pierson was called to take over the pulpit of Spurgeon's great Metropolitan Tabernacle, London, where he ministered for two years and was expected to become pastor.

Since his death, Pierson has become well known through his writ- ings. From his pen came volumes of Bible studies, volumes of sermons and addresses; he even wrote on Christian evidences (*Many Infallible Proofs*, once used as a textbook on Apologetics), works on

Hermeneutics (one volume similarly used in a Bible school for a text in that area), biographies (e.g., *Life of George Müller*), books on the Christian life, and not least, a large number of works on missions, both history and principles thereof (Robert Hall Glover in his outstanding *Progress of World-Wide Missions* cites Pierson numerous times).

And how did this notable man come to know the Lord? We take the story from *Arthur T. Pierson*, a biography by his son, Delavan L. Pierson. We read:

"At thirteen years of age Arthur left home, never again to return for any length of time. . . . Before his departure his father gave him as a life motto the injunction and promise from Proverbs 3:5–6— 'Trust in the Lord with all thine heart and lean not unto thine own understanding. In all thy ways acknowledge Him and He shall direct thy paths.' Sixty years later the son said, 'Since my father gave me that motto, no important step has been taken in my life without looking to God for His guidance and never have I looked in vain. . . .'

"Stephen H. Pierson was not a man of many words and was not given to parental lectures, but his life was clean and upright and his words carried weight. Another bit of advice he gave to his son as he sent him from home with his blessing and prayers, 'My son, you are going among strangers and will find some who think it a clever thing to call in question your faith and your father's faith and teachings. Whatever else you think or do, stand true to God and always give Him the advantage of your doubt.'

"Thus fortified, with bright prospects before him, Arthur set out for school. . . . Arthur's parents had not chosen the school hastily or with reference merely to intellectual and worldly advancement. The instructors were Christian, and the principal made it his aim to help every boy to find in Jesus Christ his Friend and Savior and then to stand by Him in every trial.

"Although Arthur had attended church and Sunday school since the age of six, and all his training and most of the influences that surrounded him had been Christian, he had never yet deliberately surrendered his heart to Christ. At school in Tarrytown there came the crisis that comes to so many boys when they first leave home, an experience which tested his earnestness and his courage. He came face to face with the question, 'Shall I seek great things for myself in my own way, or shall I give my life to God and surrender to the claims of Jesus Christ?'

"During the one year of Arthur's stay in Tarrytown, a series of special revival meetings were held in the Methodist church, and the earnest but quiet message of the evangelist made a deep impression on him. What followed is given in his own words:

"'One night I was much moved to seek my salvation. When the invitation was given, I asked for the prayers of God's people and decided to make a start in serving God by accepting Jesus as my Savior. On my way back to school I was forced to ask myself: How am I to act as a Christian before the other boys? We all slept in large rooms with five or six beds. As I went up to the ward where we slept, I felt that now or never I must show my colors. If my life were to count, I must give some testimony before my schoolmates.

"'The boys were not yet in bed and as some others had attended the meeting, the word had preceded me, "Pierson is converted." The boys were waiting to see what I would do. There was not one other Christian in the ward, and my own bedfellow was perhaps the most careless, trifling, and vicious boy in school. My first hour of testing had come; much depended on how I would meet it.

"'As I undressed for bed. I asked God for courage and then, when ready to turn in, knelt down beside the bed and silently prayed. The boys were quiet for a moment, and then a few began to chuckle, and presently a pillow came flying at my head. I paid no attention to it, though praying was not easy just then—if by prayer is meant consecutive, orderly speaking to God.

"'My schoolmates were not malicious but only bent on "fun," and when they saw that I did not move, their sense of fair play asserted itself. One of the older boys said, "Let him alone," and silently they all picked up their pillows and got into bed. I was never again disturbed when praying before my fellows.'

"The initial victory was won, and it was the man's conviction in later years that this was a turning point in his boy life.

"Immediately after his conversion, Arthur began to take his share in Christian work either by testimony in the boys' prayer meetings or by leadership in the junior society. Several of his carefully prepared talks showed thought and study quite beyond the ordinary boy of thirteen."

Pierson's story might well be concluded by an anecdote relating to later years. Hy Pickering records, "When collecting funds for a special object, a wealthy man said to him, 'If I had to preach your funeral sermon, I should take for my text, "And the beggar died."' 'I should not in least object to that,' said Pierson, 'if you only finished the verse, "And he was carried by the angels into Abraham's bosom" (Luke 16:22).'"

22

CAROLYN POOLE:
Delivered from Christian Science

Christian workers have long considered Christian Scientists among the most difficult with whom to deal. Their minds seem to be conditioned, and it seems almost insurmountable to get on the same "wave length" with them. Yet the Spirit of God is working, and souls are coming out of the darkness of that system into the glorious light of the gospel of Christ.

Mrs. Carolyn Poole is a former third generation Christian Scientist. Her testimony, condensed, follows:

"Christian Science was the most important thing in my life. I had been born and raised in it. I, too, was 'class-taught.' I faithfully served on most of the committees, including my being president of the Executive Board. I relied totally on Christian Science, never going to doctors nor taking medicine. I loved my religion, expecting to be a loyal Scientist for the rest of my life.

"Something happened to change my thinking. In 1975, while I was president of the Executive Board in a small branch church, I felt a need to know the Bible better. I believed that my religion was based on the Bible, and I knew that the Bible was one of our 'two pastors.' I realized, however, that in getting my daily lessons, I was not reading most of the Bible. So it came about that

I proposed to the church that we have a Bible study following a certain Christian Scientist's teaching on cassette tapes. Nothing came of it.

"It was during this same time that two women invited me to attend the Christian Women's Club home Bible studies. I cautiously accepted.

"At first I didn't see anything different in these studies except that the women were the sweetest, nicest that I had ever met. I felt 'good' in their company.

"After a few months the first Bible verse loomed up to disturb my thinking. My husband was reading to me from a Bible translation, Matthew 23:10, where Jesus said to call no one 'Leader' except the Messiah. This caused both of us to sit up and take notice, because Jesus and Mrs. Eddy were both claiming to be the only one to be called our 'Leader' (evidently *New American Standard*).

"A couple of months later I found myself worrying about Mrs. Eddy being frequently called 'Our revered Leader.' I looked up the word 'revere' and found that two of its synonyms are 'adore' and 'worship.' The Bible said that God is a jealous God and will not share His glory with anyone. I did not think that we should adore and worship anyone but God. I felt that it was sacrilegious to call Mrs. Eddy 'our revered Leader.'

"A short while later we started in my home a new study of the book of John. This was when the Bible began changing before my eyes. Old verses which I had read for years took on new meanings. It was as if I had never seen them before. To start with, the words came alive where Jesus said that He is the way and the only way to God. He said, 'I am the way, the truth, and the life, no man cometh unto the Father, but by me' (John 14:6).

"This reminded me of what I had read in Christian Science that Mrs. Eddy is called the 'Revelator' and that Christian Science is the 'Revelation.' We were taught that you cannot know the Revelation without the Revelator. And, of course, we have to know the Revelation in order to properly understand God. In other words, we have to know Mrs. Eddy in order to know God. This meant that according to Christian Science, she is the way to God. Now Jesus and Mrs. Eddy were, once again, making the same claim, that each was the only way to God. I had the distinct impression that she had taken the place of Jesus in the minds of her followers.

"The Holy Spirit was working me over completely, because that wasn't all that broke open before my eyes. What did Mrs. Eddy say? Pouring over her statements it was quite apparent that she did not consider Jesus and Christ as one and the same. Jesus merely demonstrated the Christ idea. Another new concept about Jesus came into being. I found that John said that 'the Word was with God and the Word was God.' Then a few lines later he said, 'and the Word became living flesh.' And he said the Word, Jesus, was God. So Jesus was God. Was this just misinterpretation? According to the Bible, Jesus was God come in the flesh.

"Most important is that Mrs. Eddy said that man is sinless. If that is true, then Jesus suffered on the cross for nothing. He said, 'This is my blood which seals God's covenant, my blood poured out for many for the forgiveness of sins.' Jesus knew what He was saying, and He meant it. The Bible said that all men are sinful and come short of the glory of the Lord.

"Suddenly one night in Bible study, I saw pieces of the Bible come together. I remembered in Revelation Jesus was called the Lamb. Then I remembered that He was crucified at the time of the Passover. I found that the blood of an unblemished lamb was put on the doorposts to keep death out. God instituted the shed blood of animals as an atonement. This was continued until Jesus' blood was shed on the cross. The Bible became very cohesive.

"For a lifetime Christian Scientist these things were hard to accept. But I came to realize that Christian Science was diametrically opposed to the Bible. I found myself at the place that I had to take all of the Bible or none of it. It made no sense to do it any other way. As a Christian Scientist I could not throw the Bible out.

"I came face to face with Jesus. I had to accept Him for who He said He is, and why He came, or I had to reject Him and the whole Bible. In either case I knew that Christian Science was wrong because it claimed to be based on the Bible, yet it denied the Bible's basic doctrine. I chose Jesus. I asked Him to forgive my sins and to be my Lord and Savior. Needless to say, I resigned from the Christian Science church. I now have the comforting knowledge that when I die, I am going to a good place to be with Jesus Christ. I pray that you have the love of the truth and that you reject the darkness in exchange for the light of Jesus."

23

PAUL RADER:
Effective Evangelist and Pastor

In *Forty Fascinating Conversion Stories* I presented the story of the conversion of Charles G. Fuller, the outstanding radio preacher of several decades ago—a truly remarkable conversion and one that led to a ministry used of God in the saving and blessing of multitudes of souls. That conversion took place under the ministry of Paul Rader. But how did Rader come to know Christ as his Savior?

I well remember sitting under the preaching of both Fuller and Rader. I used to go often to hear Paul Rader as he spoke in various places in the Los Angeles area. He stood out as an effective evangelist. But he had a varied ministry. He was pastor of the Moody Memorial Church, Chicago (1914–1921) and of the Chicago Gospel Tabernacle (1922–1929), serving also as president of the Christian and Missionary Alliance (1921–1923), succeeding its founder, A. B. Simpson. He also held pastorates in Pittsburgh, Fort Wayne, and Los Angeles.

Paul Rader's story was written by another greatly-used preacher, Bible teacher, and author in southern California, W. Leon Tucker. We take Rader's conversion from Tucker's *The Redemption of Paul Rader* (The Book Stall, NY, 1916).

"Paul Rader says, 'I was born in Colorado country, and I am sure it has had a great influence on my life.' . . . Colorado having brought to the elder Rader (Paul's father) health, happiness, and usefulness, he was honored by his church. For many years he was Presiding Elder. The parsonage was filled up with Raders. His family was large and his salary was small, yet he helped each one in their education and to seek an honorable vocation, and 'how he did it,' says Paul, 'on a Methodist preacher's salary has always been to me a miracle of Grace and Goodness of God.' Rev. Rader died in 1911, at Portland, Oregon, and was, at the time of his death, editor of the *Pacific Christian Advocate*, the official Methodist organ for the great Pacific northwest.

"Paul Rader spent his boyhood days in Colorado and Wyoming. His broad shoulders, his gigantic frame, his kindly vision, all speak of the characteristics of the great West. Rader is a great-souled Christian commoner; he is the gift of God to all the people of God. He tells the story of his own conversion in the following words:

"'I well remember the time of my conversion. I was nine years of age. My father was preaching at Cheyenne, Wyoming, where he was missionary to the Indians. There were soldiers in the house that night from Fort Logan and at the close of father's sermon, as it was the custom among Methodists, he asked S. A. Bright to give the invitation. There was real conviction of sin that evening, of which I was very conscious. I made my way to the altar. A dear saint who was known as Brother Corey said to me, "Why Paul, you love the Savior, don't you? Well," said he, "you are all right."

"'I can remember that the cloth was worn from the buttons of his vest, and the tin, over which buttons were made in those days, was exposed. Something whispered into my very soul, "God sees what you have done and what you are as easily as you see the tin on those buttons." I rose and went back to my seat, and still under conviction I went to my room, fell on my knees, and was sobbing when a little later my father made his way to my room and kneeled down beside me and put his big arm around me and said, "Now my boy, let us tell Jesus what it is," and kneeling there beside me he drew a simple illustration of how the blood of Christ can take away human guilt, and then and there I yielded myself to Him and was a new creature.

"'A joy filled my heart. It was an overflowing, outgoing joy to such an extent that I crept up into my father's lap as he sat on the bed, and there we rejoiced together, while he sang sweetly and passionately a verse of an old hymn.

"'Only three days before, I had gone to a trial where father was a witness. He told me what put the fellow's sin away and how the judge had pronounced the verdict, and his sin was put away by having it judged. He told me how sin would have to be judged unless Jesus took the judgment. Three days before that, something had happened. I had done something Mother had told me not to do, and I was up against it and knew I was up against something else. Father had grasped a whip and put it into my hand and taken off his coat and said, "Somebody has to be punished for this business. I think it would be a great deal better if you would whip me, than for me to whip you." I would have cut my hand off before I would hit him, but he told me I had to. After I had laid it on the third time I said, "Ain't that enough?" He said, "What do you think? Would you have been punished enough?"

"'He took that whipping to show me the Gospel of Jesus Christ, and that night it was very easy to show me the way to Jesus. He said, "Paul, Jesus took the whipping for you and took death for you." I never preach a similar sermon without saying what Father said to me. Listen! Jesus has taken the judgment for you, and you don't have to be judged if you will only believe Him. He loved you enough to bare His own body on the cross and take the nails in His hand and the spear in His side and endured that pain until He was dead and had paid the price of death and of sin for you.

"'It was mighty easy for my father to lead me to Jesus, and he showed me that and then asked me if I believed it. I did. And he said, "Wasn't it all over when you whipped me? Do you think about it now?" "Only to thank you," I replied. "That's what you want to do with Jesus," he said. And a thankfulness and tenderness came into my heart, and I was genuinely converted, and the next morning I knew it, and the next day, and on through the days.'

"Those who read this story of Paul Rader's conversion in the arms of his old father may well long that again we might have a type of Christian fatherhood that could throw arms about a child and lead that child to Christ. The embracing arms of a Christian father are unescapable."

24

DANIEL ROSE:
Jesus, His Messiah and High Priest

D aniel Rose is from the family that established the well-known Rose Exterminator Company. During World War I the government had great warehouses where stores which included food for the troops were kept. But these warehouses were plagued by rats. After some unsuccessful attempts to get rid of the pests, the call went out for someone to contract to keep the storehouses entirely free of rats. The Rose family accepted the challenge and, through the measures they developed, were wholly successful and thereby became wealthy. But because they were Jews, the senior Mr. Rose was given by some the epithet "rat-killer Rose."

Daniel Rose was a short man, slow of movement, with a subdued smile on his face, always pleasant and gracious, but above all the love of God radiated from him. He was highly respected by all, and he actively and generously promoted witness to the race of ancient people from whom he sprang.

The story of his conversion is taken, abbreviated, from a booklet which he wrote and freely distributed.

"I was born of Jewish parents who were strictly orthodox and very religious. My father had a deep hatred for Jesus Christ, and naturally the name conjured up in my mind all the persecutions of my people for centuries past, and I, too, hated Him.

"Because my father was religiously orthodox, I had a great desire to know more about the God of Abraham, Isaac, and Jacob. But it was always knowledge *about* Him that I sought; I was not learning to *know Him*. With religious zeal I always observed the feast days and holydays. . . . We were very worldly—drinking, attending theaters, and continually using profanity.

"It was my habit to go to a questionable theater on Sunday evenings. En route to the theater I always passed a certain church from which strains of music floated forth to touch my sinful heart. As time went on, I had a longing to stop in to hear more of the hymns that reached my ears as I passed. Finally, I tossed all objections to the winds and I, a Jew, entered a Christian church. I loved singing, and I soon found myself joining in the songs; but always when I came to the name of 'Jesus Christ,' I tried to cover it and would pause while the others sang it and would then rejoin them.

"My sister and her husband moved to an apartment house in another city, where in a neighboring apartment lived a Hebrew Christian and his wife. They lost no time in speaking to my sister about their Savior, but she resented their efforts and began to dislike them. Friends came often and stayed late proving over and over again from Old Testament passages that Jesus of Nazareth was indeed and in truth the long awaited Messiah of Israel. And day after day the Spirit of God gently spoke to my sister until finally on one glad day, she came to fully realize that her true Messiah was this One who is called the Lamb of God who takes away the sin of the world. And opening her heart to Him, she came into the peace and joy of true salvation.

"She wrote me a letter telling me of the wonderful change that had come into her life. I lost no time telling her she was old enough to know what she was doing, but that, as for me, I was born a Jew and would die a Jew and would never change my religion. . . .

"My sister would lay one hand on my wife's shoulder and the other on mine and present to us the claims of Christ from the Old Testament—our Jewish Bible. I was under such deep conviction that I begged her to discontinue, as I could neither eat nor sleep. The old Jewish customs and traditions die hard, and it is not easy to turn from a background of centuries of bitter hatred for an alleged impostor and at once to accept Him as God Himself and to worship Him as God.

"I finally reached the point of saying to myself in desperation, 'I must do something—either accept Christ or reject Him. I can't remain neutral.' I went into my room, closed the door, dropped to my knees, and said, 'O God, the God of Abraham, Isaac, and Jacob, I want to know the truth. If Jesus Christ is Your Son and my Messiah, I will accept Him, but show me the truth.' Like a flash, God's Spirit bore witness with my spirit, and the truth was borne upon me with deep conviction that Jesus Christ truly is the Messiah for whom every faithful Jew waits, and I accepted Him then as my Savior from the penalty of all my hated sins.

"The floodgates broke, and my soul was released from hell! I arose shouting and praising His name. The bands of sin had been snapped asunder, and I was born into the kingdom of God—one of His children—no longer a slave to sin. I was forever free.

"Since I have found Jesus Christ to be the Messiah and High Priest, the Savior who saves His people from their sins, I have had a deep and abiding peace which the world cannot give and which nothing can take away.

"Let me assure you that you, too, can find this peace as I did, if you will fall on your knees and pray to God. . . ."

25

HARRY SAULNIER:
"Unshackled"

The long popular radio program "Unshackled," from Chicago's famed Pacific Garden Mission, has been heard across the nation and, in fact, around the world. And wherever it went, the name of Harry Saulnier became familiar. The man became a legend in his time. For, indeed, Harry Saulnier was recognized as not only the spark behind "Unshackled's" well-known dramatized stories of remarkable skid row conversions, but also as the untiring power behind the noteworthy expansion and spiritual usefulness of the mission itself.

To the possible neglect of his family and the undermining of his health, Harry Saulnier devoted himself to the mission he loved and superintended, both day and night, for more than forty years. Not alone as an administrator and promoter, but he stood out as an indefatigable personal worker, taking time out to quietly lead individual souls to the Savior. And he held that as supreme for the eighty-some workers under him.

As the best-known rescue mission in America, if not the world, under Saulnier it did not rest on past laurels—such as the conversions of notables like Billy Sunday and Mel Trotter—but upon its continued usefulness in reaching the lost and helping large numbers of them to become rehabilitated, taking responsible places in society.

Every man's conversion story seems a bit different. And that is true of Harry Saulnier's. We take it largely from *Hallelujah Harry* by Ken Anderson (Pacific Garden Mission, 1977).

"Though he sprang from a family of staunch Presbyterians, Harry himself sums up family faith with, 'Like the Bible says, my parents had a form of godliness, but they never talked to me about really knowing Christ.' . . .

"Nothing in Harry Saulnier's childhood played so large a role in the shaping of the man as the sorry failure of both home and church to meet his spiritual needs. . . .

"The Saulniers were Sunday regulars. Their church was an imposing edifice with a worshipful sanctuary. The stained glass windows, the sound of the organ, the choir, the preaching—all filled a sensitive child's exploring mind with a blur of questions. Home scarcely seemed the place to ask these questions. Except for church attendance and the customary display of a family Bible, the Saulnier family was about as secular as the household of any nonbeliever. . . .

"Young Harry was the kind to look up into the sky at night and wonder about the stars and to see a bird in flight as an object of created beauty. He was even the kind to study his Sunday school lesson. Sunday after Sunday, as he grew older, one all-encompassing question began to form in his mind. He searched for its answer on the pages of the lesson and listened for it in the words of his teacher. He also listened to the morning sermons, all in vain.

"At the age of five, he summoned courage to lift his hand during a Sunday morning class session. 'Yes, Harry?' the teacher responded, pleased with this youngster and prone to see any student's question as a compliment to her teaching ability.

"'Who is Jesus?' the boy asked simply. The teacher's face went blank, then flushed. She completely lost her train of thought in the lesson.

"'Well . . . uh . . .' she stammered for words. Harry waited. 'We'll talk about it next Sunday,' she finally managed to say. But she didn't bring up the subject the next Sunday, nor the next.

"'Never once,' Harry himself says, 'not in all the years I attended Sunday school and worship services, did I ever hear the

Gospel in that church. They didn't speak out against the Gospel. I suppose they may have been in favor of it. But they sure never preached it or taught it.' He grew to manhood, took his place in early adult society, remained faithful to the church and consistent in attendance—but with his question unanswered. . . ."

In Chicago Harry found employment with the Commonwealth Edison Company and rapidly moved up. "Work at the generating station became intensely demanding, allowing increasingly little time for any male chit-chat, but there were times when the men slipped into more quiet areas to study diagrams and double-check work. They happened to be in such circumstances one Friday near the close of the work day. 'How do you spend your weekends?' a friend named Vic asked nonchalantly.

"'Well, Sundays I go to church.'

"'Where?'" Saulnier told him.

"Vic smiled warmly—Vic Cory who would one day found the precedent-setting publication firm to be known across the world as Scripture Press.

"'It's kind of unusual, anyone around this place talking about church,' Harry said, anxious to find out what this Cory fellow had on his mind. 'I go to North Shore,' Vic continued. 'We have a Fisherman's Club I thought you might enjoy.' Fisherman's Club? For a moment Harry had visions of sitting out in the rain in a rowboat, casting endlessly for blue gills. He never cared for fishing. . . .

"Harry and Vic became close friends. For the most part, they only saw each other at work. On a quiet job, over lunch, Vic chatted about happenings at church, especially the Fishermen's Club. 'But I don't remember him actually asking me about my own spiritual condition,' Harry remembers. 'I think he made the same mistake a lot of people make today. He felt I was a believer because I didn't smoke or drink or join in with the immoral conduct of some of the other guys.' And yet there was that unanswered question and the silence of the Sunday school teacher.

"Vic did share so much of his Fisherman's Club experiences, Harry got to thinking. Like, 'I told this guy that anybody would call the derelicts on Skid Row lost souls, but the most upright man in Chicago, if he's never been born again, is just as lost as one of those derelicts. *There is no difference*, the Bible says, *for all have sinned and come short of the glory of God.*' Slowly, like water eroding granite, the Word of God began edging into Harry Saulnier's heart. Slowly, but surely.

"Meanwhile, Harry maintained near perfect attendance at his church. 'I think the preacher was a good man,' he says. 'He may even have been a godly man. But as I look back now, it seems he kept preaching around the Gospel. He didn't deny the New Birth. He just didn't proclaim it.'

"There really wasn't any likelihood that Harry would become an evangelical Christian, a born again believer in Jesus Christ. That is except for Vic Cory. . . ."

"Just now he was trying to cope with life as it measured out for him personally, a good job, the church, loyal and wholesome friends. In many respects he was the center of attention in his own personal world yet could not ignore the gnawing emptiness."

About that time, Dr. John Roach Stratton, pastor of Calvary Baptist Church in New York City, was conducting afternoon and evening meetings in Vic's church. Vic urged Harry to attend. Harry managed to get off and take in the meetings. He heard the Gospel presented clear and plain.

"Harry Saulnier had never heard such words—never in all his life. Instead of quieting his troubled heart and mind, however, the speaker's message became like a wind against a raging fire. But no invitation was given for those who might want to receive forgiveness and peace—not that afternoon, not following the message of the evening.

"Harry stumbled out of the church, hesitating outside for a moment in the hope of someone offering to help him. No one offered. He made his way home.

"'When I got to my room,' he recalls, 'I dropped to my knees and the best I knew how to do, called upon the Lord.' Determined to find the joy and peace others talked about, he remained on his knees. He fell asleep, kneeling at his bed. 'I woke up about five the next morning,' he remembers, 'still kneeling by my bed. My knees were numb. My shoulders ached.' And his heart was full of discouragement for, though he had called upon the Lord, he could feel no difference. He dressed and went to work.

"But that very noon after gulping down his lunch, he took the New Testament he carried in his overall pocket and began reading in the Gospel of John. He had read this before but now it was a brand new book to him—fresh and alive—like a window thrown open. He read and heard no audible voice, but yet it was as though the Book spoke aloud, verse after verse."

Verses like John 3:14–15; 4:14; 5:24; etc.

"The next day Vic Cory invited him to the Fisherman's Club at the church. In that famed church where he had previously so yearned for someone to inquire about his spiritual condition, one of the men walked up to him and bluntly asked, 'Do you know the Lord, Brother?'

"'Yes,' Harry said. Just one word, but with so simple an affirmation of honest faith, the assurance of his salvation surged into the young man's heart. On the simple articulation of the word 'yes,' Harry Saulnier experienced what the Apostle wrote about in Romans 10:9–10, *'If thou shalt confess with thy mouth the Lord Jesus . . . thou shalt be saved'*."

That did it; the transaction was complete.

Hereafter Harry Saulnier would be the instrument to lead others more directly to the assurance of salvation for which he so long struggled.

Taken from the book, *Hallelujah Harry* by Ken Anderson. Copyright © 1977, Pacific Garden Mission. Used by permission.

26

THE REV. RUDOLPH SCHMITT:
From Night Club to Gospel Ministry

W e could not get better words to introduce this story than those coming from Dr. Oswald J. Smith of Toronto, Canada. He declares, "We have known Rev. Rudolph Schmitt, a missionary evangelist, and his wife, a gospel singer, for many years. They came here to the Peoples' Church several times and left a very vivid impression on all those who listened to them. . . . We are glad that Rev. Schmitt publishes his testimony, and we expect that God will make special use of it. Thus we consider it to be a privilege to recommend it." The testimony follows, excerpted:

"Both of my parents were Catholics, and I was brought up in strict Catholic faith. When I was three years old my father died; at the age of seven I lost my mother. This situation brought me to where my grandparents raised me to young manhood. Both of them were very kind to me. I finished my school years there. As is the custom, I had to be in church every morning at seven o'clock and went into the school building at quarter of eight. As everybody else belonging to this faith, I thought this will certainly do and is a life according to God's commandments. Nobody every told me that I would have to receive Jesus Christ as a personal Savior into my heart and soul in order to be redeemed.

"An uncle of mine wrote to me from America inviting me to

139

come and stay with him. I sailed for America. These relatives were very much concerned about me and did all they could for me, but after six months my uncle died quite suddenly. . . .

My friends advised me to accept a job as a violinist in a night club. For two years I was able to work with a leader of a small orchestra who happened to be very nice and instructed me some more in that line of band music. After working with him for two years, I set up my own band and had orchestras for 16 years. I made twelve West Indies cruises. Each cruise lasted 23 days. I had the band on the ship. I crossed between America and Germany aboard the steamer *America*. By that time my desire to sail the seas had been satisfied. Once again I turned to nightclub work.

"One evening I played a well-known, semi-classical song. Suddenly a lady in the audience with a very beautiful and splendid voice began to sing along. The audience applauded so loudly that this lady had to sing about 3 or 4 more songs. She told me she needed a job, and I was able to place her in a nightclub close to the one where I had the orchestra. In the course of time we got to know each other quite well, and in the end we decided we were meant for each other and got married. We earned a lot of money together.

"But my wife felt homesick for her mother who was still in Germany. We decided to have her come to us. She came, a very fine mother indeed, so we called her 'Momma.' My wife was happy now having Mother with her. But Momma was not just like any other woman; she was a true child of God, a witness for her Lord Jesus. It was she who for the first time in my life introduced me to Jesus by showing me the Bible and told me wonderful stories that were in it. She would always end by saying to both of us, this Jesus you have to accept into your heart personally. Momma did not like our life in a nightclub at all. But for us, it was *The Life*.

"Often we noticed that Momma had wept before breakfast. I told her, 'Momma, what are you crying about? You can stay with us the rest of your life; no more worries for you.' But she said, 'Rudy, you don't understand.' She asked me one day if she could say grace aloud at the table. I answered, 'Of course you can.' Then she did not thank God for the food only, but along with her prayer she mentioned my name and my wife's for salvation. This made me feel terribly uneasy, but I did not say anything about it.

"Momma discovered on the radio the voice of Charles E. Fuller. For me it was just more religious stuff of which I thought I had enough. About three years later, after listening to Dr. Fuller one Sunday, my wife broke out in tears as Dr. Fuller gave the invitation to accept Jesus Christ as personal Savior. I asked her, 'What is the matter?' She said, 'You wouldn't understand.' I took my hat and walked out.

"I came home late one evening and asked my wife for details concerning the afternoon. She said, 'Today I have handed over my heart and life to the Lord Jesus Christ; I am a child of God now. You can do whatever you like, but from now on Momma and I will pray for your salvation.' Sundays she would go to church now with Momma, and I was left home alone. I did not like that at all but did not say anything.

"Momma, who was an aggressive type, said to me, 'Why don't you come along to church just for once?' Since I had said, 'Momma, you can have any wish,' I did not want to go back on my word. But I said to her, 'Remember you said *only once*; I will go but only once.' To this day I thank the Lord that He had a good servant behind the pulpit who really preached a gospel message. It hit my heart. When I left the church, the pastor said to me, 'Will you come back again?' I replied, 'I will be back next Sunday.' For the next six months I did not miss a service.

"I made real good money, so my wife and I went to the great opening of a 'Victory Center.' There were no sermons preached, and yet there was the best preaching I have ever heard—*just personal testimonies*. Men and women of God gave testimony of their new life in Christ Jesus. The first one was president of a savings bank in New York. He held at one time the title of 'International Bank President.' He came to the platform and started his testimony by saying, 'With all the titles I have ever had, I cherish only one, *Just a sinner saved by grace.*' This cut right into my heart.

"Then a lady, one of the richest, who belonged to the upper class, told how she had promised her godly mother that she too would accept the Lord Jesus as her personal Savior. But she waited and waited and suddenly her mother was taken from her. Then she said, 'When they lowered mother's body into the cold ground, I broke down, and there gave my heart to Jesus. From now on no more cocktail parties, no more nightclubbing, but my life shall count only for my Lord and Savior, Jesus Christ.'

"Again I was hit in my heart. No longer was I a happy person with the Christians nor with the unbelievers. I was in between; I was miserable. What an awful condition to be in. I was hoping for a closing prayer so I could get out of that place. But the moderator announced, 'No one leave; the tables are set for all of you with coffee and cake. Just enjoy yourselves.'

"As we all went into the adjacent room, I thought, nothing can happen now, no invitation was given, that I like.' An ardent young man with a heart of gold came to our table. Looking at Momma he said, 'You are a Christian; I can see it in your shining eyes.' Momma said, 'Yes, praise the Lord.' Momma was saved under General William Booth when he held a very successful evangelistic meeting in Germany in 1890. Mother came out of the Jewish faith and led her own mother to the Lord after her own conversion.

"This fine young man at our table asked my wife, 'Are you saved?' 'Yes,' answered my wife, 'just a year.' He said, 'Praise the Lord.' And then the moment came which I did not expect. This man looked at me, pointed his finger at me, and said, 'Are you saved?' I wanted to defend myself, but God did not allow it. All I had heard about salvation reached the decisive stage. I don't know what lifted me to my feet, but I stood up and said, 'Whether I feel or see anything or not, by *faith* I will accept the Lord Jesus now as my personal Savior.'

"This brother standing next to me cried beamingly, '*Praise the Lord.*' Jack Wyrtzen, a great evangelist, came to our table and said, 'Brother you are the first one saved at Victory Center.' Three people went home entirely happy—Momma, my wife, and I. How wonderful our precious Lord led in our lives, Momma coming out of the Jewish faith, praying me through from Roman Catholicism.

"All in all I spent 16 years in nightclub work in and around New York and then became converted. When that took place I realized that I could no longer stay in nightclub work and at the same time speak for my Lord. Thus I left the nightclub once and for all. . . ." And after some Bible training, Brother Schmitt and his wife became active in evangelistic work, both in America and in Europe.

27

MENNO SIMONS:
Founder of the Mennonites

S ome of our friends among the Mennonites seem surprised that
so many of us in other groups become confused regarding the
origin of their name. Since they are termed Mennonites, it
might appear natural to assume that they sprang from someone
called Simon Menno, particularly since Simon is frequently a first
name. But the founder of their group was one Menno Simons.

Some Christian bodies, indeed, take their name from the
name—that is, the surname—of their founders, like the Lutherans.
Others, to distinguish themselves from similar groups, add a
founder's name, like the Wesleyan Methodists. Still others, like the
Swedenborgians, are known by the name of their founder, but pre-
fer another designation (in this case, "Church of the New
Jerusalem"). But for the one we now consider, the body has become
known by the first name rather than the family name of the
founder—Menno Simons.

The story of this man and how he came into the fullness of the
truth of the gospel is most interesting. We begin first with his biography by C. Henry Smith.

"Menno Simons, like his contemporary, Martin Luther, was of
peasant origin, having been born in 1496 in a little Frisian [Dutch]
village. . . . In his twenty-eighth year he assumed the duties of the

143

priesthood. . . . His preparation was enough to meet the simple requirements of a country priest. He knew, according to his own confession, no Scripture. Later in life, however, through wide reading he acquired a minute knowledge of the Bible. . . .

"As a priest Menno likely lived the life of his class—an easygoing, carefree life, assuming the burdens of his office rather lightheartedly. Like his companions, he spent his days, he says, in 'playing, drinking, and all manner of frivolous diversions.' Like them in all but one very unusual respect—he was blessed with an open mind and a tender conscience. Such being the case, he could not remain entirely oblivious to the revolutionary religious movements that were then shaking all northern Europe. . . . Quite early in his ecclesiastical career he had access to writings which were being surreptitiously circulated throughout the Dutch monasteries and among the Dutch priests in spite of every effort to suppress them.

"The seed of doubt fell on promising soil. One day while Menno was perfunctorily handling the bread and wine in the celebration of a mass, the thought flashed through his mind that this bit of bread could not possibly be the flesh of Christ as he had always been taught to believe. At first he gave the suggestion but little thought, ascribing it to the work of the devil in an attempt to lure a good man away from his faith. But it came back to him again and again. He prayed and sighed and confessed, but all to no avail. The conviction grew.

"Finally he was driven to the source of help to which he should have gone in the first place—the New Testament, which up to this time, he said, had been a sealed book to him. Here, finally, 'without any human aid or advice' he found relief from his doubts. His conscience was relieved and he was greatly encouraged.

"But once led to question the validity of a cardinal doctrine of the church, the way was opened to other doubts. Not long after this, Menno heard of the beheading at the capital city of the province of a tailor, because of rebaptism. A second baptism seemed a strange doctrine to the troubled priest. Thus far he had never doubted the validity of infant baptism. But now he again turned to the New Testament for light and was surprised that he could find no justification there for the doctrine.

"Although convinced that his church taught erroneous views on two important religious doctrines [transubstantiation and baptismal regeneration], yet Menno had no thought of immediately withdrawing from it or of laying down his priestly office. He had been promoted in the meantime to a more honorable and lucrative position, and the future seemed promising.

"It was about this time, too, that Anabaptists of various types began to appear in the vicinity. The new parish priest [Menno], who evidently had considerable ability as a speaker and writer, now eased his conscience somewhat and exercised his talents by a vigorous attack upon the latter [Anabaptists], gaining quite a reputation among his fellow priests for his ability to successfully refute them. 'The report spread far abroad, that I could readily silence these persons,' he said.

"But the troubled conscience of this sincere pastor would not permit him long to live under false pretense. . . . He was disturbed in spirit. Attracted by worldly success and at the same time convicted by a tender conscience, he evidently hoped for a time to serve both God and Mammon. Although not yet an Anabaptist, still he knew that at heart he agreed with some of their teachings. . . . His heart was sorely troubled. . . .

"A group of some three hundred Anabaptists . . . had taken refuge in an old cloister where they were attacked by a small force which had been sent against them. These poor deluded enthusiasts . . . were soon overpowered, and most of them, including Menno's own brother, were put to the sword. This catastrophe, occurring almost at his own door and claiming a member of his own family, made a profound impression upon the future leader. . . .

"Menno Simons was now ready for the final step. In the month of January of 1536, he laid down his priestly office, renounced the Catholic church, and shut the door on a brilliant career and a life of ease and pleasure. He deliberately chose instead a life of uncertainty, misery, and poverty that was constantly threatened with imprisonment, persecution, and death but was at the same time a life of loyalty to his convictions and great service to his fellow men and of peace with his God. . . . Menno Simons deliberately chose the way of the Cross. For the rest of his days he remained an outlaw, a wanderer upon the face of the earth. . . .

"This converted parish priest, it will be observed, arrived at his conclusions and convictions through a gradual process, by his own volition and as a result of an independent study of the Scriptures."

Another historian, Harold S. Bender, also portrays the soul struggle in Menno's conversion with the ensuing blessing:

"In extremity of soul, Menno turned to God with sighing and tears, pleading for grace and forgiveness, pleading for a pure heart and courage to preach His holy name and His Word in all truth. In his own account of his conversion Menno describes his change of heart in the following words: 'My heart trembled in my body. I prayed to God with sighs and tears that He would give me, a troubled sinner, the gift of His grace and create a clear heart in me, that through the merits of the crimson blood of Christ He would graciously forgive my unclean walk and ease-seeking life and bestow upon me wisdom, candor, and courage, that I might preach His exalted and adorable name and Holy Word unadulterated and make manifest His truth to His praise.' The Lord was gracious unto him, the decision was made, and Menno went forth with a sense of divine mission to a new life. . . . What is important to note is that once Menno was stirred, he was moved to the depths of his nature, and from that decision once made he never turned back. The change was so deep, so thorough, so complete, and gave him such a sense of divine mission, that he was enabled by the grace of God to be an inspired leader, a mighty tower of strength to his bitterly persecuted people. . . ."

Chambers Encyclopaedia says of Menno, "He was a man of gentle, earnest, modest, and spiritual nature, with no trace about him of the wild fanaticism of the earlier Anabaptists."

And the *Twentieth Century Encyclopedia of Religious Knowledge* presents this summary: "Menno's significance is . . . he voluntarily became the shepherd of those needing guidance, knowing well that he chose a life of constant danger and risk. Thus he saved and purified a movement which now soon became known as 'Mennonite.' Through this courageous act and his devoted life, a witness of the Reformation for a brotherhood and a Christian way of life was preserved which have meanwhile become quite generally recognized as an integral part of Protestantism."

28

BILL STILES:
Last of the Jesse James Gang

A s a young believer in the middle 1920s, one Sunday morning I went down to a slum area mission. I felt mission work was a great form of Christian service and testimony to what God could do. Casually remarking to the mission superintendent that I would be glad to help in any way I could, I was almost taken off my feet when he immediately requested me to take a men's Sunday school class that morning. I had never taught *any kind* of a Sunday school class before!

In being presented to the circle of eight or ten men well past middle age, the one introducing me to the group said, "You will have to speak loudly, for old Bill over here is somewhat deaf," and he pointed to an elderly man with a drooping mustache and a weather-beaten face. It was not until after I had taught this, my first Sunday school class, that I learned that "old Bill" was actually Bill Stiles, the last living member of the notorious Jesse James gang. Crime, prison, and final release were now all behind him.

From a tract that I picked up not long afterward, many copies of which I gave out, this is the story of his conversion, as he told it.

"My criminal life began back in New York as a pickpocket when I was 14 years of age. I had Christian parents and a good home. My father was a practicing physician. They did all they could for me, but the Devil got hold of me in some way, and I seemingly could not keep from doing wrong. They sent me into the country, but I did no better there. I overheard them talking of sending me aboard the school ship *St. Mary*, and then I ran away.

"I drifted westward and in 1876 joined the James' gang with the Younger brothers and was with them in the Northfield robbery. I escaped the vengeance of the law and made my way to Omaha, Nebraska. I had served three terms of one year each behind prison bars. In 1900 I was convicted of a crime and sentenced to life imprisonment. When those doors closed upon me, it was terrible; no one can know my feelings but those who have passed through such an experience. It was a life of torture—a living death.

"On the 19th of March, 1913, I got my release from prison, and friends took me to the state of Washington where I found employment in a lumber town. A friend gave me work for two months; but when he came to me one day and said that he could not employ me longer, I knew my past had been revealed, and I became discouraged.

"At last I gave up trying to be good. I found it impossible and determined to go back into my old life of crime. I began to prepare for what I knew in the end would be the taking of life before they would get me. I was desperate, and once more the old outlaw spirit was upon me, and I was becoming a demon at heart. I went to Tacoma and Seattle and looked up some of my old pals—men who did not care for their lives. With them I planned to go back into my old work of train robbing.

"I came to Los Angeles on the 19th day of July, 1913, and began to look up this country, both along the Santa Fe and Southern Pacific Railroads, preparatory to 'striking' and then striking again. I went into the mountains for a month and drew my maps and laid my plans. I came back into the city and put my men (as they had bad records and were wanted by the police) in hiding.

"The night before the intended robbery, I walked down Main Street, thinking over my plans and the course mapped out, when I found myself in front of a mission. Just then I saw a policeman coming down the street and, naturally, feeling suspicious, I stepped inside to avoid him and walked way up front. This was the first time I had been in a church service since a small boy, nearly 44 years before.

"I did not hear much of the service, for my mind was upon the work for the next day. I felt a little uneasy, for I had left my suitcase in my room and in it some of the 'soup' (nitroglycerine), some high explosives, and my guns. I had everything ready, and so far my plans had gone smoothly; but, as I say, I felt worried and was just getting up to leave when one of the workers came to me and asked me to give myself up to God. I told him that I did not believe in a God. The life I had lived did not allow me to believe in a God. I do not remember his reply, for when I attempted to get up, I had no control over my legs. I kept trying to get up when a woman came and sat down beside me and urged me to go up to the altar. I listened to her pleadings for a time and then consented to go, thinking it would do me no harm anyway. It was not the woman, for I had been a woman-hater since my early life; it was the power of God. As soon as I gave my consent, my legs were released, and I went up and knelt at the altar. I heard them praying, and a strange feeling came over me. It seemed as though something in my heart was loosening up. How sorry I began to feel for my past life of crime. I could not keep back the tears—tears of real repentance. I had found the Lord. Oh, what joy came into my heart!

"I went out of the mission knowing real happiness in the Lord, for I was conscious that my sins were forgiven. I could not go to bed for joy but walked the streets for hours. I forgot all about the train robbery I had planned for the next day—forgot the suitcase and guns.

"Next morning after my conversion, I told my companions what I had done, and they said I was nutty. I told them if I was, I hoped God would give me more. I then separated from my old pals, and they went their way. I am sorry to say that two of them have paid the death penalty already—one was killed in a raid in the North, the other in Arizona.

"For a number of days I sat in the mission, I was happy for the first time in my life. Finally I began to come to myself and to think about the law, knowing that I was liable to be arrested, for I had revealed my past life. I thought about going away but was held from doing so by a feeling of love, and such delight was in my heart and soul that I knew I was in the presence of God's Spirit. The peace of God flooded my soul, I was a new creature in Christ Jesus.

"I broke my mother's heart and sent her to her grave in disgrace.

A dear old father and sisters and brothers have all passed away, and their last thoughts were of me. That heart of mine was as hard as stone; nothing ever melted it, and my soul was black with many a crime, but the Lord took me and washed me as white as wool. I know that a man who has lived the life I have can never *reform*, but through the power of God he can be *transformed*."

29

PHIL THATCHER:
Prisoner Turned Prison Worker

Phil Thatcher and I were born the same year in the same state, California. And we were both preachers' kids. I did not know this when he came to speak at the college where I was teaching and where I was privileged to entertain him in the college dining room. But I do remember some interesting discussions we had. And I knew the prison chaplain, John Dunlap—we had both been missionaries in the Philippines—the chaplain who encouraged him so after his conversion following a life of crime and grueling prison terms. Since his release and full pardon by then California Governor Earl Warren, Thatcher has done a great work among delinquent youth and has been welcomed to address prisoners in some of the largest penal institutions across the nation.

One crucial difference in our backgrounds was that Phil had the great misfortune to lose his father at an early age. But it is best to let him tell his own story, as presented by Dorothy Haskin in *Under Arrest*.

"I remember when I was a little guy and was arrested for the first time. I was eleven years old and living in Sacramento.

"There were six of us children. Mom was a pretty, slim woman, with eyes that looked at a fellow as if she had faith in him. She was

151

still in her teens when she and my dad were married. I know they were happy together, and his death was a shock to her. In her early thirties, with six children, she was not trained to earn a living for us. She had to work as a domestic. With Mom gone all day long, I had the inward feeling that no one cared what I did. I was really looking for someone to take Dad's place and love me like he did, only I didn't know what it was that I wanted. . . ."

He stumbled into crime, repeated petty offenses. "At the age of eleven I was sent to a reformatory." He escaped several times. Later he involved himself in more serious crimes. Then came the inevitable pay-off.

"I was sentenced to serve from one to ten years in San Quentin. I was on my way to the Big House! The sheriff had handcuffs fastened around my wrists and hurried me into a car. When I sat down, he put irons on my legs, heavy things that cramped my muscles but saw to it that I didn't try to jump out of the car.

"Why did I have to be the one who was going here, while the man at my side was free? He was a cop. Why? I didn't really know the answer. I knew only that, no matter how hard I tried, I couldn't straighten myself out. . . .

"One day I was handed a visitor's pass; I walked into the visitors' room, and there sat my dear sweet Mom. How grand to see her! But what a place for a man's mother to come to see him! . . .

"As she looked up at the machine gun pointed in our direction, she said, 'Son, when are you going to quit this life and really live?' Mom went on, telling me God through Christ could make all things better for me. She had told me the same thing so many times. But something in my heart was still stubborn and hard. I listened. I nodded. I loved her, but I didn't make any promises. . . .

"Soon I was working in the officers' and guards' mess. My first job there was helping Tom Mooney peel spuds. Tom Mooney and Warren K. Billings had been convicted of placing a bomb at the corner of Stewart and Market Streets in San Francisco during a preparedness parade, July 22, 1916. . . .

"I was released after spending four years and three months in San Quentin. . . ."

Again the downward path and the pay-off.

"Only sixty days had passed since I had been released from San Quentin. I was thirty-one and had spent as much time in confinement as out since I was eleven years old. Soon, in handcuffs and leg shackles, I was headed toward one of the toughest prisons in the United States. It was called 'bloody Folsom' on account of a riot that had recently taken place there. My hands and feet had been shackled by the sheriffs, but I was held even more firmly by Satan.

"'Well, here's your new home,' said one of the sheriffs. 'We shouldn't have any trouble with you for about twenty years.' I snarled back at him an unprintable answer. He gave me a push toward the gate, and it was lucky for him that my wrists were still shackled. . . .

"I thought back to my days as a little guy and of the prayers that Mom had taught me at her knees. 'Now I lay me down to sleep. . . .' I prayed that little prayer, and somehow Mom felt closer. . . .

"I had been in Folsom six months when one night I returned to my cell to find an old Bible lying on my bunk. It had been thrown in by one of the trusties. I picked it up, stared at it, threw it on the shelf above the door, and cursed the trusty who had thrown it in. That, I thought, was the end of that Bible.

"The next day I hit harder and cursed louder, but nothing stopped the memories of my childhood. I kept remembering the verses Mom had taught me, and I could almost feel the touch of her hand upon my head as I had knelt beside her in prayer. My defense was gone. There was a gnawing inside me, and I returned to my cell a miserable man.

"As soon as I thought Scotty [his cell-mate, who was later executed] was asleep, I crawled out of bed, picked up the Bible, stood close to the door where a sliver of light crept in, and read the Book. Later, when I climbed back on my bunk, my memory went back to my childhood, seeking to find the place where I turned off the right path.

"There was only one good thing about that cell in Folsom—it was small, cold, and the air was musty and stifling, but there was nothing to distract my attention. I spent most of my spare time reading the Bible. Night after night I plowed my way through. At last I reached the New Testament where I read about the Lord Jesus hanging on a cross on Calvary's hill.

"One evening I found a letter from Mom on my bunk. She wrote as she always did, of the Lord Jesus who had died for my sins. As usual, I tore up her letter, but the words she had written burnt in my soul. Now, when I reached for the Bible, my hand shook. And a few days later upon returning to my cell, I threw myself on my bunk and cried and cursed and cried and cursed some more. The battle within me went on until the lights went out, and God brought my whole rotten life before me as a picture on a screen. Through all memories I could see Mom and my sisters praying for me—Mom's prayers that I had tried to push aside but that followed me all through my life.

"Finally, I could stand no more. Within myself I cried, 'O God, if there is a God, if you are the God that my Dad preached and my Mom prayed to, please show me.' A man can't talk to God like that and mean it without an answer. I got my answer.

"I seemed to hear the verse, 'The blood of Jesus Christ His Son cleanseth us from all sin.' Somehow I cried, 'Oh God, if You did this for me, what can I do?' A voice way down inside of me said, 'Phil, just ask Me to forgive you.' And so, somehow, in that cell, with only the dim light from the hall lighting it and with Scotty snoring on the bunk below, I prayed, 'God, be merciful to me a sinner, and save me, for Jesus' sake, Amen.'

"It had been a struggle, but I was at peace with God and with a world with which before I had been at odds. Soon I fell into a peaceful sleep, to awaken to the clanging of the gong. But this morning I had a smile on my face and a joy in my heart. I was a new creature in Christ.

"About ten days after my conversion I went to the chapel. A group of men were gathered there with Chaplain John Dunlap, who was teaching them out of the Bible. I dropped into a bench and listened. After the class was over, the chaplain came to me and said, 'Who are you? I've never seen you around before. Are you a Christian?' 'Yes.' The fellows looked at me as if they thought I was crazy. Most of them had seen me box; they knew the tough clique that I had hung around with, and they didn't understand this switch of mine. But Dunlap is a great guy. He shook my hand and said, 'Well, God bless you!'"

30

NARAYAN TILAK:
High Caste Hindu Converted

Narayan Tilak was born in India, springing from a family of high caste Brahmans. He has been recognized as a great intellectual, a nationalist patriot resisting Western tendencies, and as a highly acclaimed poet. Volumes of his verses have been published, and his hymns are widely used in Indian churches—as entirely native products, they are decidedly preferred over translations of Western hymns. When his conversion became known, it created a sensation throughout India.

One source says, "Writing was his great ministry; his hundreds of *bhajans* [hymns] gave the Marathi Church a worthy Indian medium of praise . . ." (*New International Dictionary of the Christian Church*, Douglas). And Kenneth Scott Latourette reports, "He believed that the rebirth of India to hope would come through submission to Christ. He . . . composed Christian songs in his native tongue" (*History of the Expansion of Christianity*, vol. VI).

Tilak's own story is told at length in the book, *I Follow After* (Oxford University Press, England), and in abbreviated form in *From Brahma to Christ* (NY, Association Press, 1956) by his wife. She was also from a high caste Hindu family, and her experience, too, is deeply moving since his religious pilgrimage estranged them for many years, and her own unsteady quest caused her great suffering at the hands of her unsympathetic relatives.

In the Introduction to the last named book, Canon Stacy Waddy of England points out, "It is not easy for others to realize the Himalayan difficulty of a Brahman's mind opening to new light and of his breaking out of the prison cell of caste pride into the world of Christian freedom." He further says that both Mr. and Mrs. Tilak were "Brahmans, born and nurtured in strict households where the laws of religious observance and purification were meticulously honored, and to lose caste was the greatest of all disasters. But after five years of separation passed in tears and prayers, his wife rejoined him with their son, and later she too became a Christian."

Mr. Tilak thus tells of his conversion:

"Was I not the sworn enemy of this Christ and His followers? With this hand, now so eager in His service, how many papers have I scribbled off in the heat of my scorn for Him? This tongue, which today is always ready to witness to the one great mercy of Christ, has heretofore poured what unrestrained contempt on that Holy Name? In former days did anyone think, or even dream, that I would become a Christian? Could anyone have conceived that this man, so proud of the Hindu religion, would propose to forsake it and glorying in the Bible, abandon himself to the will of God?

"Nevertheless this, my pride perished, and today I stand like a small child before God holding the hand of Christ. Is it any wonder that people should see this and be astonished? I myself am astonished at myself. I had no intention of becoming a Christian. What overflowing pride and arrogance were lodged in my breast! . . .

"I formed the habit of regarding all subjects with an open mind. According to my ability, I gave myself up to the study of religion and philosophy. At Nagpur I found much knowledge about Hindu Vedas and the science of Supreme Spirit manifested in the Individual Self. For three years I dwelt in that ocean of meditation and spiritual knowledge.

"I began to study the lives of the founders of different religions. With many of them I did not agree. However, in Gautama Buddha I found one to my liking, and I thought of copying him except for his mistakes. The astonishing thing is that not even into my dreams did the Bible or Christ enter, the chief reason being the extremely simple language of the Bible. It has become the very birthmark of a Brahman that he will only turn his mind to incomprehensible subjects or those which will exercise his utmost intelligence.

"I never met a Christian preacher. I had not even read one or two pages of the Bible. I had only heard and read plenty of things against it. I used to think the only difference between Christians and idol-worshipers was in their eating and drinking customs. . . .

"The raja of the small state of Rajnandgaon offered me work, and I boarded the train. But when I came to the carriage, a European was sitting there; I expected the usual experience of being turned out. Nothing of the sort happened; on the contrary, smiling a little, he made room for me.

"My companion in the compartment was extremely polite and gentle, so that anyone would have been drawn toward him. I had with me only one book to read, a well-beloved book of Sanskrit poems, and we talked for a long time on poetry and poets. He knew a little Sanskrit and was familiar with its literature.

"Slowly he turned the conversation and questioned me about my opinion of the Christian religion. We continued talking for a long time, and he said, 'Young man, God is drawing you. Study the Bible. Apply yourself wholeheartedly to the life of Christ, and in truth you will become a Christian.'

"Considering this an exceedingly rash speech, I cursed it in my heart. Lastly he prayed, took out a New Testament, and gave it to me. I disliked the book at sight; however, I promised to read it, not thinking there would be any meaning in the book, but only for the sake of gratifying this good man. We said an affectionate farewell. It is a strange thing that to the end neither of us asked the other's name or dwelling place.

"At Rajnandgaon I was teacher, clerk of the Royal Court, and government clerk. For a man with a passion for reading, there was little there to occupy the mind, and all my most beloved Sanskrit books were in Nagpur. This forced me to keep my promise. I decided to read the book through from beginning to end, marking the passage worthy of more thought. But I only got as far as the Sermon on the Mount.

"It became impossible to leave these jewel-like sentences, so filled with love, mercy, and truth. The most difficult questions of Hindu philosophy found their answer in these chapters. I was astonished to see problems like that of rebirth fully resolved, and filled with desire for more knowledge of Christ, I read eagerly on to the end. A Christian police superintendent gave me a little book and tracts. My hunger for a knowledge of the life of Christ grew. I found the information I wanted. Now, one after another, God sent answers to my prayers. I was dumb with astonishment. My mind became riveted on Christ.

"After some months I began to feel that in spirit I was a Christian, but love of my people and love of honor led me into temptation, and I ignominiously denied it. It is difficult for others to understand the persecution that must be endured when his caste brothers find out that some high-caste Hindu has become a Christian. Though God may have been far from me at other times, in times of trouble He was near me, as a mother is near her child night and day when it is ill and crying. From all kinds of trouble He saved me. I lost my work; I had to go away leaving my only child. My wife clings to her own people. But God has not deserted me. . . .

"I was resolved to make it known to the world that I was a Christian. This fact was published in the *Indian Christian* magazine, and my greatest desire was fulfilled. May God be praised; I was baptized in Bombay in the American Mission Church. The prophecy made two years earlier in the train by that stranger had come true. God had drawn me to Himself, and with overwhelming loving-kindness He guides forward His weak child."

31

H. C. TRUMBULL:
Many-Sided Servant of God

There was a day when *The Sunday School Times* was the leading evangelical or Bible study magazine in America. Its circulation was unprecedented and probably not surpassed then or since. The one who made it that and long edited it was Henry Clay Trumbull.

But Mr. Trumbull was not only known as an editor and author (his biography lists by title 33 books written by him); but also as an army chaplain (during the Civil War, being once captured and imprisoned); then as missionary, archaeological explorer (he is credited with discovering the site of Kadesh-Barnea); as an educational lecturer (although he had no earned degree!—delivered the Lyman Beecher lectures at Yale University); and other noteworthy activities.

Trumbull became so widely recognized, indeed, that he was called upon to offer the prayer at the burial of General (ex-President) U. S. Grant, under whom he served (and, incidentally, springing from the same ancestry). Interestingly, Trumbull entertained in his home on the same occasion, two famous "Marks": Mark Hopkins, noted president of Williams College, and Mark Twain.

As to *The Sunday School Times*, he enlisted as contributors such men as college presidents, eminent seminary professors, and on occasion, governors of States, U. S. Senators, and once a communication from Rutherford B. Hayes while he was President of the United States, also from ex-President U. S. Grant.

Another whose outstanding knowledge he made use of was the great Orientalist, Prof. A. H. Sayce of Oxford University, who said of him, "Dr. Trumbull was essentially a man of power, both moral and intellectual, and exerted a deep and abiding influence upon men of very different minds and points of view. There were things about him which always struck me more especially—his strong common sense, his religious and moral earnestness, and his capacity for continuous and conscientious work."

And Dr. Arthur T. Pierson said of him, "A flaming evangelist he was; intense, earnest, and fluent, we used to hail H. C. Trumbull's visits with delight. All the neighboring pastors used to welcome his coming and vacate their pulpits to give him room. What struck me in this dear friend of my youth was his singular power of marshaling facts. He was a field marshal in the realm of oratory. But there was nothing artificial. His enthusiasm was contagious. He moved his audiences. What he afterward did by the pen, he had begun to do by his tongue in earlier days when he swept like a flame through the East." No wonder that D. L. Moody had him at his famous Northfield conferences.

In *Great Personal Workers*, Faris D. Whitesell presents as the first eminent example, this man, of whom he says, "H. C. Trumbull was a man among men. He was equally at home with the common people or with the world's great leaders of his day. . . . None has ever set forth the basic principles for fruitful personal evangelism more clearly, wisely, and acceptably than he. . . . Out of the multitude of his evangelical activities for Christ, he had no doubt that his personal evangelism was the most profitable of them all." Whitesell then cites Trumbull's widely acclaimed book, *Individual Work for Individuals*, in which Trumbull strongly pressed the matter of each soul having a personal experience of becoming a true child of God.

How, then, did he himself come to experience that saving work of God? The story is told in *The Life Story of Henry Clay Trumbull*, by Philip E. Howard, from which this account is taken: "The Trumbulls attended the Congregational Church. Henry had never seriously faced the question of his acceptance of the Savior though he was a pupil in the Sunday school. . . ."

Then, when he was out and making a living on his own, and after various successful activities are related, many pages later we read:

"Great revivals of religion swept the country. A new evangelistic method emerged. Classsical illustrations and ornate phrases were tabooed. The preacher took on greater boldness of utterance; he adopted what were called 'new measures.' And among all the evangelists none was more radical, more startlingly clear and original in his simplicity and forcefulness than Charles G. Finney.

"In the winter of 1851–1852, upon his return from England, Finney was in Hartford conducting a series of meetings. Young Trumbull made no effort to attend these meetings. In the preoccupation of his office work he hardly gave them a thought, assenting tacitly to the disesteem in which such doings were held by his everyday companions.

"Letters from home told of a revival of interest in religion in Stonington [his hometown]. One after another of his companions there had confessed Christ, but the news from home made no special impression upon him as affecting him in any way. One noon, however, as he was returning from dinner to his railroad-office work, he found at the post office a letter from an intimate Stonington friend, E. D. Stanton. He had heard from this friend only a few days before concerning the revival at home. He opened the letter, read a few lines, saw that it was a personal appeal to him, and at once thrust the letter into his pocket, saying to a companion, 'I think there must be a big revival in Stonington if it has set my old friend preaching to me.'

"Young Trumbull reached the office which was on the third floor of one of the station towers, but he passed up the stairs to the fourth floor and entered a small map-closet where he shut himself in. The letter had been speaking to him ever since he saw its first lines. He now opened it and read it through:

"'I have been too long silent. The prevalence of a deep religious feeling in this community has, to some extent, opened my eyes to my former shortcomings and led me to consider what was my duty in using my influence, small as it may be, to direct the attention of any of my friends to the consideration of eternal things. Often have I felt like speaking to you on this subject, but as often have timidity and fear kept me back. We have been intimate friends for years. It seems to me that thus what you might have considered from another an act of intrusion, you will consider from me an evidence of my sincere regard and my earnest desire for your good.'

"Then Stanton urged him to seek the Savior and find peace in Him, and finally he said, 'Let me beg you by the remembrance of our friendship, but more than all, by the regard for your own good, think of these things. . . . I have now tried to acquit myself of a duty too long neglected. . . .'

"Henry Trumbull was touched beyond expression by his friend's letter, and even before he had read it through he was on his knees, brokenly asking God's forgiveness for his heedless past. . . . Then, after what must have been a night of strange and unwonted thought-experiences, he set pen to paper and told his mother the story she had longed that he might someday tell:

"'You are doubtless aware that there has been for some time past a very general and unusual interest upon the subject of religion in this city and that protracted meetings have been held. I have only known of the continued progress of the revival by the laughter and ridicule of "Father Finney and his theater" continually kept up by my fellow boarders. . . . Being alarmed because I was not alarmed, I began to think upon what course I should pursue. I yesterday received two letters, one from Edmund Stanton being a long letter upon the subject of religion, urging me by every consideration to turn my attention to the subject. It has caused me to pause in my present course and induce me to determine that I will now give my attention to the important subject of my eternal salvation. . . .'"

A warm, rejoicing letter came back from his mother, and then a word from his father, "'. . . I hope you will avoid all metaphysical inquiries into the philosophy of the sinner's redemption or its *modus operandi*. It is a matter between the individual and his God and Savior who is always near, always ready, always willing to hear even the most broken, incoherent petitions of the humble and contrite. . . .'"

Shortly he wrote to his mother again, "'Last evening I was again released from the office early in the evening and again went to hear Mr. Finney. He makes no appeals to the feelings, no appeals to our fears. He presents a subject calmly and rationally; he appeals to the reason and understanding rather than to the passions. . . . This appeal from one who described my feelings so exactly and who evidently understood my difficulties and my doubts apparently opened my eyes and gave me a glimpse of the truth and of my duty; and as I offered up a mental prayer that Christ would accept of my offer of my life and strength to be devoted to His service and glory, it did seem as if I had found the true entrance to eternal life.'

"Then, with the evangelistic spirit breaking down the barriers of doubt within him, he gives expression to the reality of the new life that was in him, as he exclaims, 'Oh, how I trust and hope that the revival may continue its good work and that many others may be brought to Christ.'"

Thus, with a good beginning, Henry Clay Trumbull was set to go far in the service of Christ.

32

COUNT NICOLAUS LUDWIG VON ZINZENDORF:
A Nobleman Forsakes All for Christ

There are not many of whom it could be said, "[He was] the individual who did the most to advance the cause of Protestant missions during the course of the eighteenth century," and, "[He left an] influence that in many respects equaled or excelled that of his personal acquaintances, John Wesley and George Whitefield." Yet that is what is said of Count Nicolaus Ludwig Von Zinzendorf (Ruth Tucker in *From Jerusalem to Irian Jaya*).

Indeed, of this man born a nobleman (1700–1760), it is further said, "He corresponded and conversed with kings and princes that he might bring them to the Savior, and he followed the Indian savage into his wilderness that he might tell him of Jesus. Earthly possessions, honors, and fame were to him as nothing in comparison with Christ" (Schaff-Herzog four-volume *Encyclopaedia of Religious Knowledge*). Zinzendorf was a man of many talents—pastor, teacher, theologian, missionary, hymn-writer, liturgist, and administrator.

Mention having been made of John Wesley, it is of interest to note his first contact with Zinzendorf. Immediately after Wesley's noted Aldersgate Street experience, commonly recognized as his conversion, we read, "It was characteristic of Wesley that he should start at once for the Continent to see Count Zinzendorf. . . . He was confirmed in his belief that their [Moravian] foundation doctrines contained the secret of peace and power" (C. Silverster Horne, *Popular History of the Free Churches*). It is also interesting to note that later, Wesley translated into English a number of Zinzendorf's hymns. Perhaps the best known is, "Jesus, Thy Blood and Righteousness, My beauty are, my glorious dress."

Although thought of by Americans as an old-world European, Zinzendorf came several times to this continent. Besides earlier visits to the West Indies, he spent about two years here preaching, teaching, evaluating, organizing, etc. His "going out on missionary journeys to the Indians extended as far as the Wyoming Valley, Pennsylvania, where, in all probability, he was the first white man to pitch his tent" (Schaff-Herzog). Rather significantly, it was he who gave the name to what has since become no mean city: "On Christmas he named the settlement which Moravians were beginning to effect in Pennsylvania, Bethlehem" (Walker's *History of the Christian Church*).

Reference being thus made to missionary activity, it is doubtless in this area, beyond other accomplishments, that Zinzendorf is chiefly remembered today. The afore cited Ruth Tucker says of him, "One of the greatest missionary statesmen of all time. . . . He founded the Moravian church, but above all else he launched a worldwide missionary movement that set the stage for William Carey. . . . In the two decades that followed, the Moravians sent out more missionaries than all Protestants (including Anglicans) had sent out in the previous two centuries"! And Robert H. Glover speaks of their "having three times as many members in their foreign missions as in their home churches. Such on the part of a community so weak in numbers and wealth . . . is traceable in large measure to the mighty spiritual impulse imparted by that remarkable man, who, as their leader, set before them an example of such unqualified consecration of every talent, faculty, and resource he possessed to the Christ whom he adored. . . . They have been taught prompt obedience to the call of God to go anywhere and with emphasis upon the worst and hardest fields as having first claim" (*The Progress of World-Wide Missions*).

As an example of the last feature, Arthur T. Pierson calls attention to one being asked if he would go to bleak Greenland. "Certainly," was his reply. "When?" "Tomorrow." "How will you live?" "We will build houses and cultivate the land." "But," objected the Count, "there is no wood to build with." "Then we will dig in the earth and lodge there" (*The New Acts of the Apostles*, and J. A. Graham's *Missionary Expansion Since the Reformation*).

And they did indeed go to Greenland.

Turning to his personal life, we learn that Zinzendorf's father came from a line of noblemen; he had been Prime Minister of the Saxon Court, a godly man, but died six weeks after his son's birth. The boy was raised by a pious grandmother, a Baroness.

The story of his vital conversion may be found in J. R. Weinlick's *Count Zinzendorf*, given in Zinzendorf's own words as taken from *Old Landmarks* (translated by F. F. Hutten):

"Up to my tenth year there was more care bestowed upon me by way of shielding me from evil influences and fostering in my heart the work of grace than would have been possible anywhere except in a well-ordered church of Jesus Christ. I can say with truth that my heart was religiously inclined as far back as I can recollect, and even at such times when refractory, proud, and peevish humors seized upon me, and vain and foolish pride of rank beset me, my heart's affections never departed from my Savior. . . .

"During my stay with my revered grandmother, two circumstances occurred which decided my whole career. When I was six years old, my preceptor [tutor], after a service of three years, took leave of me. In doing so he spoke a few words to me about the Savior and His merits and in what sense I belonged to Him and to Him only. These words made so deep and lively an impression on me that I fell into a long protracted paroxysm of tears, during which I firmly resolved to live for Him alone who had laid down His life for me.

"My dear Aunt endeavored to keep me in this frame of mind by often speaking to me loving and evangelical words. I opened all my heart to hear, and we then spread my case before the Lord in prayer. I was not in the least afraid. I freely told her all about myself, both bad and good. This was of so great benefit to me that I could never forget it. This confidential interchange of thought and feeling prompted all my endeavors in later years.

"In my eighth year an old hymn which my grandmother sang on retiring to rest led me into a long train of thought as I lay sleepless on my couch. The most subtle and refined speculations that atheists have ever invented spontaneously arose in my mind and threw me into no little perplexity. This, however, had the good effect that, when in later years these same cavils and speculations were again thrust upon me, they seemed to me to be very shallow and superficial and made no impression whatever on my mind."

Much later Zinzendorf referred to that which was the basis of his assurance: "As I came to look closely at my own conversion, I noted that in the necessity of the death of Jesus and in the word 'ransom money' there was a special secret and great depth, where though the philosopher trips, revelation stands immovable. That gave me an insight into the whole teaching of salvation. . . . The propitiatory sacrifice of Jesus became our special and only testimony and remains so to eternity."

The story has frequently been related of how the young nobleman on a grand tour of Europe—the accepted course for budding young aristocrats—one day casually entered a gallery and came to stand before a noted painting of Christ in the agony of His suffering. Underneath it were the words, "All this I did for thee; what hast thou done for Me?" This so arrested his attention that he lingered long before it as its impact sank deep into his conscience. So moved, he went forth to give, regardless of the cost, his life, talents, and possessions to the cause of Christ, spurning a life of statecraft as urged by those close to him. This turning point constituted his dedication to service rather than his conversion.

Following through, it is said that "all the seductions of Paris and the other cities of Europe which he visited did not draw him from Christ" (George Smith, *Short History of Christian Missions*). Indeed, he came to turn over most of his large estate to persecuted and hounded brethren seeking refuge. It became the famous Herrnhut, he himself being the spiritual overseer, the center of the worldwide missionary activities of the Moravians.

In *Nineteen Centuries of Missions* (W. W. Scudder) we read, "He gave his property to the work, and he became a guide and director of the most self-denying service missions have ever known." And our Encyclopaedia (Schaff-Herzog) says, "He was more than a century in advance of his age. He came forth victorious from every attack that was made upon him and from all persecution."

Zinzendorf is reported in some ways to have been rather eccentric, and he apparently held a few minor religious views which would seem strange to us today. Some found him hard to get along with, but he was notably adept at reconciling differences between antagonistic parties.

Zinzendorf spent some time in London where he was well received. He was at home with the upper classes as well as the lowest. "In Berlin he secured the king's good will and labored among the nobility with so much success that forty-two carriages were once counted waiting at his door during a religious service" (Duffield). When he died, he was "honored by thousands in many parts of the world. Thirty-two presbyters and deacons from Germany, Holland, England, Ireland, North America, Greenland, and other countries bore his remains to their last resting place" (Schaff-Herzog).

May God raise up in our day men with such consecration, vision, and readiness to follow through for His glory.

33

JOHN WANAMAKER:
Department Store Founder

Anyone spending time in Philadelphia will become familiar with the great Wanamaker Department Store, the first real department store in America. It was founded by John Wanamaker who also took over a failing store in New York and built it up to be a leading store of its day there. The *Encyclopedia Americana* tells us that John Wanamaker "began his business career at 14 as errand boy in a store. . . . He soon became the foremost merchant of Philadelphia." Indeed, he became known widely as "the Merchant Prince."

Having been active in the public life of Philadelphia, he was made Postmaster-General in the cabinet of President Harrison, where he served with distinction. What is not so widely recognized is that, as the Encyclopedia tells us, "he organized a small Sunday school which became one of the largest in the United States, of which he was for many years the superintendent." Through the years his Christian testimony has been undimmed.

John Wanamaker told the story of his conversion to the eminent revival song leader, Charles Alexander:

"A salesman asked me if I wouldn't go to his church. I was at a prayer meeting there one night; it was a quiet, old-fashioned meeting. A handsome old man of about seventy years got up and, in the gravest way, said that he was just waiting for God to take him; that he had lived his life; that God had been good to him; and it was all summed up in the statement that religion was a good thing to *die* by.

"I sat back, and I always had a great fashion of talking to myself. I said, 'Well, old man, you can't touch me. You have lived your life. You haven't any sympathy with a big boy. It has passed over my head!'

"Soon after, a young man got up. He was perhaps thirty-five, and he said:

"'You have heard an old man tell you that religion was good to die by. I want to tell you it is good to *live* by. I have just begun the Christian life. Two years ago I was converted. I had just begun business, and I had had a prejudice against religion. They told me that a man could not smile or do anything that would make him happy. You see, I was deceived about that. I am a great deal happier since I became a Christian because it settled things. I am a better businessman. A great load has rolled off my heart, and I can give myself more to my work.'

"I listened to him, and I said to myself, 'There you are. You want to be a businessman. He tells you that religion is good to live by. Another man tells you that religion is good to die by.' Then I said, 'Suppose you were in court and heard statements like that. Would you believe them?' 'Yes,' I replied to myself. 'Well,' I said, 'do you intend ever to become a Christian?' 'Yes.' 'Well, if it's a good thing, why don't you be it right away?' I said, 'Yes, I *will*!'

"I waited in the meeting until everybody went out except the janitor and the old minister, and as he came down the aisle, he met a country boy coming up, and I was that boy. I simply said to him, 'I have settled it tonight to give my heart to Jesus Christ.' And he reached out his hand and said, 'God bless you, my son; you will never regret it!'

"I didn't wait to get some feeling. I accepted the *fact* that I was a sinner and that there was a Savior for sinners, and I came to Him simply on the proposition that the gift of God is eternal life."

34

JOHN WESLEY:
Founder of Methodism

The name of John Wesley is too well known to need much introduction. Remembered as the founder of Methodism, he became famous for his statement, "the world is my parish," and, indeed, his influence was worldwide. Along with his brother, Charles, the great hymn writer, the two "are jointly commemorated in Westminster Abbey" where "a wall medallion displays their twin profiles."

So universally recognized is John Wesley that even secular authorities give generous space to him. My Funk & Wagnalls *New Standard Encyclopedia* (vol. 25) reports, among other things, "During his itinerary of half a century 10,000, 20,000, and even 30,000 people would come together and wait patiently for hours until the great evangelist appeared on horseback upon the scene. . . . Until his seventieth year all his journeys were done on horseback, and he rode 60 or 70 miles day after day, as well as preached several times. During the fifty years of his apostolate, he traveled 250,000 miles and preached 40,000 sermons. Yet he managed to do a prodigious amount of literary work. The list of works is too long for insertion here. . . . He further prepared numerous collections of psalms, hymns, and sacred songs [a number translated from other languages], with several works on music and collections of tunes." Another source says, "The number of works he wrote, translated, or edited, exceeds two hundred."

All that is to say nothing of his organizing, administrating, appointing, and presiding over workers; establishing chapels, schools, and orphanages; and preparing manuals for his steadily increasing Methodist societies in the British Isles and even in America.

While a student at Oxford, where he received his master's degree, he and his brother Charles joined what was dubbed the "Holy Club." They were not ashamed of the designation. They followed rigorous religious exercises, self-sacrificially engaged in many charitable works, and by numerous other strenuous endeavors sought to gain salvation, only to find that the salvation of the soul is not won by good works.

To further advance their well-meant desires, the brothers sailed on a mission to America, thinking, alas, such labors would bring the reward sought. We take the amazing but oft-repeated story from *The Life of John Wesley* by C. T. Winchester:

"It is significant to notice that Wesley's reasons for going to Georgia were essentially the same as the reasons he had alleged a year before for staying in Oxford. In a letter written four days before he sailed, he says explicitly, 'My chief motive is the hope of saving my soul.' In the wilds of America, removed from the pomp and show of the world, with little opportunity for foolish and hurtful desires, he will be free, he thinks, from most of the temptations that daily beset him in Oxford. . . .

"On the ship was a company of twenty-six Moravians. As the slow weeks of the three months' voyage wore on, Wesley saw in them a deep and quiet faith, an undisturbed serenity of spirit such as he coveted but could not attain. When, at the close of a day's storm, an immense wave broke over the ship just as they were at evening song, and the English passengers were screaming with terror at the prospect of immediate shipwreck, the Moravians continued their singing as calmly as if they had been in the chapel at Herrnhut. 'Were you not afraid?' asked Wesley of one of them the next day. 'I thank God, no,' was the reply. . . .

"On landing, Wesley sought out the Moravian pastor of Savannah, Spangenberg, to ask advice as to the work he was to undertake. To his surprise, Spangenberg said, 'My brother, I must first ask you one or two questions. Have you the witness within yourself; does the Spirit of God bear witness with your spirit that you are a child of God?' and added, as Wesley hesitated, 'Do you know Jesus Christ?' Wesley could only say, 'I know He is the Savior of the world.' 'Friend,' replied Spangenberg, 'but do you know He has saved you?' and when Wesley replied, 'I hope He died to save me,' pushed the further question, 'Do you know, yourself?' 'I do,' answered Wesley, but adds in his account of the interview, 'I fear they were vain words.' . . .

"The example and teaching of the Moravians unquestionably convinced Wesley of the possibility of an assured personal religious experience to which he was a stranger. During his stay in Georgia Wesley was a High Churchman, with a longing after Moravian quietism and assurance.

"Perhaps the deepest reason for Wesley's lack of hold upon the community [in Georgia] is to be found in the fact of his own spiritual restlessness during those years in Georgia. His almost feverish activity, his anxious performance of all outward duties, his extreme personal asceticism, all may indicate that the religion he was urging upon others had not yet brought entire satisfaction to himself. . . .

"The keenest cause of disappointment [after his return to England] Wesley found in his own spiritual condition. By his own confession, two years and a half before, he had gone to Georgia to 'save his own soul,' and his own soul was not saved. The entries in his Journal give a clear statement of the nature of the poignant dissatisfaction with himself. 'I went to American to convert the Indians, but O who shall convert me?' Five days later, 'I who went to America to convert others was never myself converted,' and he brands himself, 'a child of wrath,' and 'heir of hell.' . . . 'The Faith I want is a sure trust and confidence in God, that through the merits of Christ, my sins are forgiven, and I reconciled to the favor of God.' . . .

"It was not until the 24th of May, 1738, that he believed himself to have attained the faith for which he was waiting. The passage in the Journal is a classic in the annals of Methodism: 'In the evening I went very unwillingly to a society in Aldersgate Street where one was reading Luther's preface to the epistle to the

Romans. About a quarter before nine, while he was describing the change which God works in the heart through faith in Christ, I felt my heart strangely warmed. I felt I did trust in Christ, Christ alone for my salvation; and an assurance was given me that He had taken away my sins, even mine, and saved me from the law of sin and death.' It was much to have gained that composure of spirit he had so long desired. . . .

"It is true that the Wesleys did teach, all their days, that, in a very real sense, men might know their sins forgiven. They preached a religion that could not only be professed and believed, but *experienced*. Therein is the secret of the success of the whole Methodist movement."

Showing the wide recognition given the conversion experience of Wesley, I find in the modern *The Columbia-Viking Desk Encyclopedia*, in a short article, the following: "At a religious meeting in London, Wesley experienced an assurance of salvation through faith in Christ alone. This conviction formed the basis of his message to the world."

From the longer biography, one more citation, taken from pages much later, is most fitting: "The one proof of a divine sanction upon his work he found in that absolute and often sudden change of temper and desire which turned thousands of those to whom he preached from vice to virtue, from a life of sin to a life of righteousness. This, call it conversion, new birth, or what you will, was an indisputable fact. It was such a miracle as had attended the preaching of the Gospel in every age, and a miracle that the Christian Church could never afford to disavow or depreciate.

35

WILLIAM WILBERFORCE:
Emancipator, Reformer, Philanthropist

Throughout a large portion of the world Wilberforce is recognized as principally responsible for the abolition of slavery in England, preceding and setting the example for the same in America.

In England the infamous slave trade was long carried on to the great profit of men in high standing and influence in Britain, thus making its abolition seem well-nigh impossible. Yet in the providence of God, a man of strong character and true Christian faith, though long suffering from ill health, fought through all obstacles until his cause carried the day. Wilberforce first saw the slave trade halted (1807), and then three days before his death (1833), word was brought to him that the bill he sponsored completely freeing the slaves passed its second reading in Parliament (fully enacted a few days later), thus freeing 700,000 slaves at a cost of $100,000,000 (*Wycliffe Biographical Dictionary of the Church*). So appreciated was he in all this that he was granted the high honor of being buried in Westminster Abbey, where a statue was also erected in his memory.

Rather interestingly, a letter since referred to as "a now famous letter" (*Eerdmans Handbook to the History of Christianity*), is quoted by C. S. Horne (*A Popular History of the Free Churches*) as follows: "The very day before John Wesley the aged sank into final unconsciousness, he wrote a letter to William Wilberforce which surely deserves to be called the most remarkable dying testament ever penned, 'My Dear Sir: Unless Divine Power has raised you up . . . I see not how you can go through your glorious enterprise in opposing that execrable villany, which is the scandal of religion, of England, of human nature. Unless God has raised you up for this very thing, you will be worn out by the opposition of men and devils; but if God be for you, who can be against you? Are all of them together stronger than God? Oh, be not weary in well doing. Go on in the name of God, and the power of His might, till even American slavery shall vanish away. That He who has guided you from your youth up may continue to strengthen you in this and all things is the prayer of dear sir, your affectionate servant, John Wesley.'"

While Wilberforce is remembered chiefly as the great English emancipator, as most any secular encyclopedia will bear witness, that was by no means his only work of distinction. As evidence of his true Christian character and the fruit it produced, the *Encyclopaedia Britannica* (11th ed.) reports, "Wilberforce published *A Practical View of the Prevailing Religious System of Professed Christians . . . Contrasted with Real Christianity*, which within half a year went through five editions and was translated into French, Italian, Dutch, and German. . . . He occupied himself with a plan for a religious periodical, the *Christian Observer*. . . . Interested himself in . . . the foundation of a project for opening a school in every parish for the religious instruction of children, . . . and a method for disseminating, by government help, Christianity in India."

In those days little lads were pressed into service as chimney-sweeps, ordered to descend grimy, sooty chimneys for cleaning at the peril of their health. Wilberforce saw the need and advocated "relief for boy chimney sweeps" (Eerdmans). In another direction he was one of the first to associate himself with the newly formed British and Foreign Bible Society. No wonder W. B. Riley, in listing some of the outstanding benefactors of mankind, headed the list with this man: "What apostles of humanity have made such real and lasting contributions to the happiness of mankind as William Wilberforce . . ." (*The Bible of the Expositor and Evangelist*, N.T. vol. 7, p. 175).

Of great interest is the story of how, as a young man, Wilberforce came under the influence of gospel truths and then how his widowed mother sought to tear him from it by involving him in the frivolous social life in which she herself was active.

Even *Chambers Encyclopaedia* sets forth some of this, "Wilberforce, at the age of 9, on his father's death, was sent to where, under the care of a pious aunt, he ran the risk of becoming a Methodist. But his mother did not approve of a serious education and removed him to where the religious impressions he had received were soon dissipated by a life of gaiety. He was quick and spirited and fond of society in which his lively conversation and musical talent made him a great favorite." But some good seed had been sown.

Further details are given in a biography by Garth Lean, *God's Politician* (London, 1980). We read, "When his father died, he went to live with his childless uncle and aunt, William and Hannah Wilberforce, . . . friends of George Whitefield. . . . Hannah often took William to hear the evangelical sermons preached in the parish church. His heart was won by what he heard, and particularly by the sermons and stories of the Reverend John Newton, a former slave ship captain who was a frequent visitor. 'I reverenced him as a parent when I was a child,' William said later in life.

"William's mother became thoroughly alarmed at her son's letters, fearing that he was 'turning Methodist.' She was religious in a formal sense but loved social life and had the fashionable hatred of 'enthusiasm.' She took the coach to London to rescue her only son from what she considered 'little less than poison,' while [his wealthy] Grandfather Wilberforce vowed that 'if Billy turns Methodist he shall not have a sixpence of mine.' William's uncle and aunt protested, but his mother . . . bore William away.

"William felt the parting from his aunt and uncle deeply. 'It almost broke my heart,' he said later. His letters to them are full of his lonely struggles to retain his faith in the face of concerted opposition from his home and his new headmaster. They had to be written in secret.

"Meanwhile the gaieties of Hull were gradually having their

effect on his naturally vivacious spirit. 'The theater, balls, great suppers, and card parties were the delight of the principal families of the town,' he wrote later. 'This mode of life at first distressed me, but by degrees I acquired a relish for it. . . . I was everywhere invited and caressed; my voice and love of music made me still more acceptable. The religious impressions which I had gained at Wimbledon continued for a considerable time, but my friends spared no pains to stifle them. I might almost say that no pious parent ever labored more to impress a beloved child with sentiments of piety than they did to give me a taste of the world and its diversions.'

"The social whirl had captured him. . . . He wrote, 'If I had stayed with my uncle I should probably have become a bigoted and despised Methodist; yet to come to what I am now, after so many years of folly as those which elapsed between my last year at school, is wonderful.'"

Reaching maturity, Wilberforce won an eminent seat in Parliament and became a close friend and advisor of Prime Minister Pitt. Winston Churchill, in his *History of the English-Speaking People*, notes that Wilberforce was "the only person ever to enjoy Pitt's full confidence" (Lean, p. 34). But deep, hidden forces were at work.

Quoting Lean again, "The future was bright with opportunities. Life, too, was infinitely enjoyable. He was privy to most Cabinet secrets and welcome in all the grandest houses. It was at this moment that a series of events took place which were to transform his prospects. They shattered his aims and left him a new man."

No less than the *Encyclopaedia Britannica* takes note of this. "A journey to Nice . . . led to his conversion to Evangelical Christianity and the adoption of more serious views of life. The change had a marked effect on his public conduct."

Back to Lean: "The process began when he took his mother and sister to spend the winter on the Franco-Italian Riviera. . . . The influence of his Wimbledon uncle and aunt was now well buried. . . . Across France he ridiculed with all his bitter skill the views of the Methodists. . . . At Nice, Wilberforce idly picked up a book, *The Rise and Progress of Religion in the Soul* by Philip Doddridge. This study, punctuated by frequent reference to passages from the Bible, brought Wilberforce to an intellectual assent to Biblical Christianity. . . . Gradually, intellectual assent developed into deep inner conviction. . . .

"He danced, sang glees, and ate and drank himself through enormous social occasions. The thought pressed in upon him, however, that 'in the true sense of the word I am no Christian.' Unseen by the crowd, a sharp conflict raged inside him. He had begun to question the propriety of his own behavior. . . . Soon he was overcome with spiritual anguish. 'It was not so much the fear of punishment by which I was affected, as a sense of my great sinfulness in having so long neglected the unspeakable mercies of my God and Savior.'

"Again, 'I was filled with sorrow. I am sure no human being could suffer more then I did for some months.' 'The struggle was sharp, as it must be for anyone who, for the first time, honestly reviews his life and motives in the light of Christ's demands. . . .'

"These thoughts really crystallized his inner battle. If he was to become a Christian, he must be fully at God's command. Would that mean his losing his friends, of whom Pitt was the most valued, and his popularity, laying aside his political and social ambitions? He had to choose between Christ and the world. 'Pitt,' said Wilberforce years later, 'tried to reason me out of my convictions, but soon found himself unable to combat their correctness.'"

So, regardless of the price, Wilberforce fought on. He was impressed that he should confer with his old acquaintance, John Newton. John Legg, in *The Footsteps of God*, relates some of the circumstances: "Such, however, was the contempt of fashionable society for evangelicals that Wilberforce took the most elaborate precautions of secrecy and even walked twice round the square before he could bring himself to knock on Newton's door.

Lean's biography bears this out. "It was perhaps natural that the successful politician should find it hard to approach the man who typified the faith and affection he had known as a boy and then rejected to the point of ridicule. But the real reason of his hesitation was an unwillingness to identify himself with the most militant Christianity of the day. It proved to be a turning point." And the turning point brought him through to victory. He wrote in his journal, "Expect to hear myself now universally given out as a Methodist: may God grant that it may be said with truth."

But he won the full respect of his colleagues. *Chambers Encyclopaedia* reports thus on the parliamentary vote to abolish the slave trade: "It was carried by an enthusiastic majority. Sir Samuel Romilly compared the feelings of Napoleon, then at the height of his glory, with those of the English Philanthropist 'who would that day lay his head upon his pillow and remember that the slave-trade was no more'; and the whole House burst into applause and greeted Wilberforce with enthusiastic cheers."

So in the long run, the cost of being true to God brings no regrets.

Taken from *God's Politician* by Garth Lean. Copyright © 1980 by Tyndale House. Used by permission.

36

SIR GEORGE WILLIAMS:
Founder of the Y.M.C.A.

In the beginning of the Y.M.C.A. this organization was principally a soul-winning effort, one endeavoring to reach young men with the saving message of the gospel of Christ. *Eerdman's Handbook to the History of Christianity* says it was "an international organization for evangelism among young men" (p. 533). And the *Wycliffe Biographical Dictionary of the Church* says its purpose was "to win other young men to the Christian faith" (p. 436). As a side line, but only as a natural outflow of regeneration, it included the general improvement of things for young men.

And what was the Christian experience of George Williams as founder, afterward so recognized that he was knighted by Queen Victoria (hence the Sir before his name)? We begin with Harold Begbie's biography of him, fittingly titled *The Ordinary Man and the Extraordinary Thing*, "In the autumn of 1821—rather a savage and brutal period of English history—there was born a child destined to spread the influence of his personality not only throughout the British isles, not only throughout the British Empire, but throughout the whole world. . . ."

As a lad, George "went to church and heard a great many sermons and listened to a great many prayers which made no

183

impression on his mind and contributed not the smallest influence to his spiritual development. He drove his father's sheep to the moors and contracted the habit of swearing. . . .

"Little George Williams, careless of anything in the nature of religion and given to swearing, made his acquaintance with spiritual life in the shop of a Bridgwater draper [cloth merchant]. There were two other apprentices in this business, and both of them were serious lads. Their conversation, their manner of life, the whole set and purpose of their characters came to the farmer's son as a great awakening. He became vividly aware of another world penetrating and interpenetrating the world of sense, a world of which he had scarcely begun to dream. His master was a Congregationalist and insisted that his apprentices should attend chapel.

"The early spirit of Methodism was abroad, and in the Bridgwater chapel little George Williams heard sermons which deepened the influence made upon his soul by the conversation of the other apprentices. He saw that infinity separated good from evil. He became sharply sensible of the great issues of character. He visualized the two great roads on which every man that lives must make his journey to Eternity. He felt in the deepest recesses of his soul the immense separation of sin and the exquisite unifying force of love. 'I now began to pray,' he said, 'but even on my knees oaths would come to my lips.'

"A sermon in chapel determined his life. It is a case of one who had begun to seek, one who had already detected the great difference between good and evil, quietly but with an iron decision turning the direction of his inward life away from selfishness, vanity, and evil toward love, beauty, and God. There as he sat and listened to a sermon by a preacher whose very name is probably forgotten, the youth in a back pew of the chapel just simply turned his face to God and decided for righteousness.

"He said of that time, 'I learnt at Bridgwater to see the vital difference, the tremendous importance, of the spiritual life. I saw in this town two roads—the downward road and the upward road. I began to reason and said to myself, "What if I continue along this downward road, where shall I get to, whence is the end of it, what will become of me?"'

"After the service he returned to the shop, knelt down behind the counter, and, in a phrase too marvelous and beautiful in the history of mankind ever to become false or meaningless, gave his heart to God. 'I cannot describe to you,' he said, 'the joy and peace which flowed into my soul when first I saw that the Lord Jesus had died for my sins and that they were all forgiven.'

"Uncertainty had come to an end. Darkness rolled away. Henceforth he saw a straight road, a definite destiny, and a great light streaming from the kingdoms of invisible beauty."

Turning momentarily to another biography, *Sir George Williams*, by J. E. Hodder Williams, we read of Williams, "He was one of those happy men who can point to the hour and place of the changed life, of the end and the beginning. . . . George Williams is the brightest gem in the unfading crown of a simple minister of the Gospel, who, in the common round of his work, without taking special thought or making special appeal, was the means of leading him to the Master.

"Did George Williams ever forget? When riches and honor came to him it was ever one of his chief delights to help and encourage the humblest minister of the Gospel wherever he might be. . . .

"Following this unknown minister, there enters the homeland the startling figure of the Rev. Charles G. Finney, the great American evangelist. . . . To these printed lectures by Finney is certainly due much of the zeal and passion which produced the Young Men's Christian Association. . . .

"He belonged to that generation of great men who in the twinkling of an eye were born, it would seem, into the fullness of their faith. Once the decision was made, no questionings seemed to trouble him. What he believed, he believed with all his might . . . .

"George Williams was to the end strict, stern, and positive in his religious beliefs. He belonged to the old Evangelical school of thought, and he held to his creed with intensity and intense sincerity."

Returning to the account by Harold Begbie, we read of how, in a later place of employment, "George Williams found himself in that great warehouse on Ludgate Hill, one among a host of young men whose lives for the most part were as low and vulgar as it is possible to conceive. . . . Horrified by what he saw and heard, Williams looked about him for at least one or two virtuous men with whom he might share his spiritual life in this crowded scene of materialism. It was with him from the very first a certainty of God that the spiritual life is to be shared. To associate with men who loved the Way, whose hearts were consecrated to the Truth, whose souls longed forever greater indraughts of the Life, this was the peculiar genius of his spirit and the definite achievement of his great career.

"When he had found the two or three, they gathered themselves together and prayed. . . . He set his little company of faithful friends to pray for other men, the most unlikely and hardened men, and their lives were transformed. Miracles occurred in that warehouse. . . ."

And this final quotation from Hodder Williams, "It was said in after years that when he joined Messrs. Hitchcock & Rogers it was almost impossible for a young man in the house to be a Christian, and that, three years afterward, it was almost impossible to be anything else."

All this speaks for itself. This is the man to whom credit is due for founding the Young Men's Christian Association in 1844. The strength of its early days is seen by what we read of its first World's Conference in Paris in 1855 where the "test of membership, since known as the 'Paris Basis,' was adopted: 'The Young Men's Christian Associations seek to unite those young men, who, regarding Jesus Christ as their God and Savior, according to the Holy Scriptures, desire to be His disciples in their doctrine and in their life, and to associate their efforts for the extension of His kingdom among young men'" (*Schaff-Herzog Religious Encyclopaedia*, 4:2564).

ADDITIONAL BIOGRAPHICAL CHARACTER STUDIES

Mark These Men   J. Sidlow Baxter
A treasure house of Bible biographies including Elisha, Elijah, King Saul, Daniel, Gideon, Balaam, and Nehemiah. Also included are New Testament characters such as the Apostle Paul, Lazarus, the rich young ruler, Ananias, Simon of Cyrene, and many others.

ISBN 0-8254-2197-7   192 pp.   paperback

Life Verses #1—A Bunch of Everlastings   Frank W. Boreham
The first of Boreham's unique, Great Texts Series of imaginative, and dramatic sermon stories drawn from the lives of great Christians and other historical figures. A wealth of illustrative material!

ISBN 0-8254-2167-5   192 pp.   paperback

Life Verses #2—A Handful of Stars   Frank W. Boreham
Another volume of the Great Texts Series of imaginative and dramatic sermon stories drawn from the lives of great Christians and other historical figures. Boreham captures the unchanging essentials of God's Word at work.

ISBN 0-8254-2169-1   208 pp.   paperback

Life Verses #3—A Casket of Cameos   Frank W. Boreham
Another volume of F. W. Boreham's unique, imaginative, and dramatic sermons drawn from the lives of great Christians and other historical figures such as David Brainerd, George Whitefield, and Charles G. Finney. Pastors and teachers will appreciate the wealth of illustrative material; readers will be drawn to Boreham's delightful and always insightful sermon stories.

ISBN 0-8254-2168-3   208 pp.   paperback

Life Verses #4—A Faggot of Torches   Frank W. Boreham
Another volume of F. W. Boreham's unique, imaginative, and dramatic sermons drawn from the lives of great Christians and other historical figures such as St. Augustine, Richard Baxter, Samuel Johnson, and Augustus Toplady.

ISBN 0-8254-2165-9   256 pp.   paperback

Life Verse #5—A Temple of Topaz   Frank W. Boreham
The last of Boreham's unique, five-volume series of imaginative and dramatic sermons, *Life Verses* brings to light the often untold "rest of the story" of the Bible's impact on famous lives.

ISBN 0-8254-2166-7   272 pp.   paperback

The Apostles of Jesus   J. D. Jones
Dr. Jones' knowledge of human nature, principles of leadership, and how to draw the best out of people, all find expression in his timely study of the Apostles. This treatment deserves to be read carefully for we have much to learn from "The Twelve."

ISBN 0-8254-2971-4   192 pp.   paperback

David: King of Israel   F. W. Krummacher
David—a man of conflicts and contrasts. All the depth and dramatic richness of King David's life permeate this classic study by F. W. Krummacher, acknowledged by many to be the greatest evangelical German preacher of the nineteenth-century.

ISBN 0-8254-3061-5   416 pp.   paperback

Elijah the Tishbite   F. W. Krummacher
A thorough, analytical work on the character of Elijah. Here is a moving
Bible biography that will give the reader new insight into the man, his mes-
sage, and his ministry.

ISBN 0-8254-3059-3   208 pp.   paperback

Elisha: A Prophet for Our Time   F. W. Krummacher
A stimulating, fast-paced biography of one of the greatest of the prophets.
Dr. Krummacher's warmth and eloquence gives this thorough and ana-
lytical study an up-to-date relevancy.

ISBN 0-8254-3060-7   256 pp.   paperback

Chariots of Fire   Clarence E. Macartney
Drawing upon colorful yet lesser-known characters of the Old and New
Testaments, Dr. Clarence Macartney presents eighteen powerful and time-
less sermons. One of America's greatest biographical preachers,
Macartney's sermons aim for the common heart of human experience.
Each sermon contains a wealth of illustrations and quotations that add
depth and insight to the exposition. *Chariots of Fire* is eye-opening, biblical exposition from one of America's premier preachers and makes an
inspiring devotional or study resource.

ISBN 0-8254-3274-x   192 pp.   paperback

Great Women of the Bible   Clarence E. Macartney
A collection of sermons from a master pulpiteer of yesterday. Macartney's
unique descriptive style brings these women of the Bible to life and provides inspirational reading for all Christians.

ISBN 0-8254-3268-5   208 pp.   paperback

He Chose Twelve   Clarence E. Macartney
This careful study of the New Testament illuminates the personality and
individuality of each of the twelve disciples. A carefully crafted series of
Bible character sketches including chapters on all the apostles as well as
Paul and John the Baptist.

ISBN 0-8254-3270-7   176 pp.   paperback

Paul the Man   Clarence E. Macartney

Macartney delves deeply into Paul's background and heritage, helping twentieth-century Christians understand what made him the pivotal figure of New Testament history. Paul, the missionary and theologian, are carefully traced in this insightful work.

ISBN 0-8254-3269-3   208 pp.   paperback

Spurgeon's Sermons on Old Testament
    Men, Book One   Charles H. Spurgeon

One of Spurgeon's favorite presentations was the biographical sermon, drawing upon both the faithfulness and the failures of biblical characters. Includes sermons on Abraham, Moses, David, and Daniel.

ISBN 0-8254-3772-5   160 pp.   paperback

Spurgeon's Sermons on Old Testament
    Women, Book One   Charles H. Spurgeon

In this sermon collection Kregel Publications has assembled a biblical portrait gallery of Old Testament women including sermons on Eve, Sarah, Ruth, and Esther.

ISBN 0-8254-3781-4   160 pp.   paperback

Spurgeon's Sermons on New Testament
    Men, Book One   Charles H. Spurgeon

Includes sermons on: John the Baptist; the man with the withered hand; Pilate; Stephen; and Simeon, who watched for the "consolation of Israel." As always, pastors and speakers will find ample "food for thought" in Spurgeon's exposition as well as "seed thoughts" to help in sermon preparation. Christian readers will find encouragement in Spurgeon's insight into the practical issues of Christian living.

ISBN 0-8254-3783-0   160 pp.   paperback

Spurgeon's Sermons on New Testament
    Women, Book One   Charles H. Spurgeon

Includes sermons on: Mary's "Magnificant," the woman at the well, Mary Magdalene, Lydia, and the New Testament's reference to the Queen of Sheba.

ISBN 0-8254-3782-2   160 pp.   paperback

Classic Sermons on the Prodigal Son   Warren W. Wiersbe
These sermons by highly acclaimed pulpit masters offer unique insights
into perhaps the most famous of Christ's parables. These sermons will pro-
vide new understanding of the relationships between the son, father and
older brother. Readers will also be challenged to apply the wonderful truth
of the Father's love to their own lives. .

ISBN 0-8254-4039-4   160 pp.   paperback

Available from your Christian bookstore, or

P. O. Box 2607 • Grand Rapids, MI 49501-2607